History of Royal Air Force
HALTON
No. 1 School of Technical Training

The Badge of No. 1 School of Technical Training.

The badge on the front cover promulgated by AMO N 674/39 was approved by George VI in June 1939. The motto *Crescentes discimus* (We learn as we grow) appears under the familiar Beech Tree always associated with Halton. A second badge, that of RAF Halton, approved by Elizabeth II in October 1981, features a wooden propellor, superimposed on the five arrows contained in the arms of the Rothschild family to which the Halton estate belonged.

History of Royal Air Force
HALTON
No. 1 School of Technical Training

by

Paul Tunbridge

Buckland Publications Ltd.
125 High Holborn, London WC1V 6QA

ISBN 0 7212 8094 0

Printed and bound in Great Britain by
Buckland Press Ltd., Dover, Kent.

CONTENTS

LIST OF ILLUSTRATIONS

AUTHOR'S PREFACE

When I first began writing this book few thought that No 1 School of Apprentice Training Royal Air Force Halton would be closing down. The graduation of the 155th and final Entry at RAF Halton in Summer 1993 and also at RAF Cosford in Autumn the same year marked the end of apprentice training. With the ceremonial handing over of the Queen's Colour for No 1 School of Technical Training in November 1994 by RAF Halton to RAF Cosford, the complete story can now be rounded off as a definitive history.

I have, I hope, portrayed something of that light-hearted philosophy – an essential part of the 'Halton spirit' – which as well as, 'smoothing' my own stay at Halton has since RFC days been a characteristic of the Air Service. All who served in the Royal Air Force in the air or on the ground – and particularly when faced with dangerous or just impossible situations – will appreciate how much that odd hearty chuckle helped.

The story of Halton which begins with the training of Boy Mechanics for the Royal Flying Corps is part and parcel of the history of the Royal Air Force. In this way I have devoted my first chapter to Lord Trenchard since without him there would have been no Royal Air Force, no Aircraft Apprentices and no Battle of Britain – in which incidentally, at least 80 ex-apprentices were fighter pilots. The rest follows in roughly chronological order, with the detailed information given as appendices. My appended day-to-day account of Halton for instance, contains unedited diary extracts.

The excellence of the education and character moulding in the different apprentice schools, of which Halton was the largest, may be seen in the number of graduates to succeed both in the service or civil occupations. Topping the list of the 123 who made Air Commodore or higher, we find one Marshal of the Royal Air Force, 4 Air Chief Marshals, 8 Air Marshals and 29 Air Vice-Marshals (see Appendix K). Instead of asking one of these distinguished ex-apprentices to contribute the Foreword to this book, I settled for a personal letter from a pre-war Commandant, Air Vice-Marshal Sir Ranald Reid. I did so because as one of the few to have completed two tours of duty at Halton he probably knew it better than most.

Many ex-apprentices on the other hand succeeded brilliantly in their civilian careers. One entry recently commemorated its 50th anniversary with a booklet:

41st Dispersal. A very distinguished member of this outstanding entry in a personal letter summed up what Halton training had done for him:

'Looking back over my career, I think the apprentice system served me well. It would not be true to say that I enjoyed every moment of it, nor that in me it produced the best of technicians, but it turned a rather shy, quiet lad into someone capable of facing up to life and gave me the foundation on which to build a career in which I eventually became a leader, first as a Principal and then as a Chief Executive, responsible for the work and careers of many other people'.

This ex-apprentice's post-RAF career which 'took off' at Edinburgh University ended as Director of the London Chamber of Commerce Examination Board. His post-retirement activities as educational consultant includes Deputy Chairmanship of a Parliamentary Executive Committee. He believes that the RAF will in time regret having ended the apprenticeship system. He considers that 'the advent of technicians competent only in spare-part replacement technology and factory/manufacturer-based maintenance may be cheaper in peacetime, but much less effective in the emergencies of war service'.

Another member of the same entry, a doctor of philosophy and management expert, is now Senior Lecturer at a leading University. In quoting Tennyson's 'So many worlds, so much to do, So little done, such things to be', he wrote that ex-brats with experience both in the RAF and industry should present their ideas on the form future apprenticeships should take so as to 'at least plant a seed of doubt somewhere'.

On 1 December 1988, Mr Roger Freeman, Under-Secretary of State for Air, announced at Halton that, as part of the continuing process of streamlining ground training in the Royal Air Force, technical training would be carried out at RAF Cosford. Subsequently, with a view to cost saving it was decided that while aircraft engineering training would be concentrated at RAF Cosford, recruit and administrative training would be carried out at RAF Halton.

Thus the Apprentice scheme ended primarily as the result of the inevitable pressure for economies – I have shown how its existence had already been threatened in the early 'twenties with the Geddes Committee. In addition, entrants earned less and had fewer restrictions than those entering as Direct Entrant trainees. Well-educated boys preferred waiting a year or so to enter a university course. Increasingly sophisticated aircraft design necessitated less in-house maintenance, much of which is contracted out to manufacturers. Finally, the numbers who for various reasons failed to complete the demanding Halton training was undoubtedly a cause for concern.

Future engineering training in the RAF would, as Air Chief Marshal Sir Michael Armitage (56th Entry, and Patron of the Halton Aircraft Apprentices Association) explained in the summer 1993 issue of *The Haltonian,* continue in the form of a single-gate, dual-stream method of entry for Trade Groups 1 and 2.

Those entrants with four GCE/GCSE passes at grade C or higher, including maths and physics, join the Technical Entry Scheme while those less qualified can enter the Mechanic Entry Scheme. All entrants would start with a Basic Training Course of up to 35 weeks, including 7 weeks recruit training. Then after one to two year's productive service they could be selected for a further engineering course to graduate as Junior Technicians. Selected students would then be trained to BTEC Higher Certificate standard. In his view, this new 'sandwich' type course was unlikely to provide the type of leaders brought forward under the traditional RAF Apprenticeship system for younger entrants.

Perhaps I should add, as is always stated on the first page of *The Haltonian*, that opinions expressed in this book, including my own, do not necessarily represent official views.

Air Commodore G R M Reid, DSO, MC. Air Officer Commanding RAF Halton 1936-1938 – the decisive expansion years for Halton.

(Photo via HAAA)

FOREWORD

Personal letter from Air Vice-Marshal Sir Ranald Reid KCB DSO MC Commandant Royal Air Force Halton 1936-1938 (previous service RAF Halton 1921-1923).

What a lovely place Halton was, and still is. What a splendid job the ex-apprentices did in the last conflagration. Many have fallen by the wayside now. The splendid vision of Trenchard, the Father of the Royal Air Force, led to the formation of Halton. A great apprentices' three-year training scheme to provide ground crews for the superlative British Air Force, he saw as essential for this country's survival.

Halton started in 1921 with the intake of well-selected schoolboys. They came in their hundreds, school-caps and satchels and all. We received them in the hutted military North Camp (myself just back from Egypt as C.O. 47 Sqn plus some excellent young officers and NCO's). Great barracks, workshops and schools were completed for their accommodation and training in their thousands.

Without the resulting engineers and mechanics Britain could not have won the Battle of Britain and save the country from invasion. Some memories are: firstly, the excellence and keenness of the young folk in work and play; the lovely countryside, gardens and grounds of Halton Camp. The good senior staff from old Dan Scarlett[1], the ex-naval station commander (his son killed later as a senior and daring RAF commander in war); the second in command Cyril Newall[2] later C.A.S., always cheerful and efficient; Harry Beauchamp[3] the R.C. parson (monseigneur) who hunted 8 days a week they said, yet did a fine job with his young flock (Master Tring Drag Hounds) with Whaddon Chase and the Old Berkeley. Philip Sassoon the Air Minister gave Halton ponies to help form a Polo Club, and we played on the aerodrome. Many local huntsmen and horse copers joined the fun . . . That is enough from an old hand.

This harsh photocopy of a Reuter photograph (with letter 14.11.1981) may be enough to satisfy your request . . . I hope so . . . Congratulations on your varied career. It is good to see how well these young schoolboys prospered after Halton . . . Winston C. does look smug, but those beady brilliant eyes are absorbing everything, linked with the turbulent brain behind. Glad I had the honour of a handshake.

---

1 Air Commodore F.R.Scarlett CB DSO first commandant RAF Halton January 1922 to February 1924, retired as AVM in 1931.
2 Marshal of the RAF Lord Newall GCB CMG CBE AM Chief of Air Staff, 1st September 1937.
3 The Reverend Henry Beauchamp, served at Halton 1919-1939.

ACKNOWLEDGEMENTS

I should like to express my appreciation to Group Captain Joe Ainsworth CEng, MRAeS, MBIM, of the Halton Apprentices Association for his recommendation and support. I would thank ACM Sir Michael Armitage KCB CBE (56th Entry) for permission to quote from his Trenchard Memorial Lecture 'The Legacy of the Trenchard Apprenticeship Scheme' presented at the Royal Aeronautical Society, Halton Branch on 19 April 1990.

The Haltonian, and predecessors, as reference sources, have proved invaluable. My thanks go first to its Editor, Bill Kelley (56th Entry) and the RAF Halton Aircraft Apprentices Association, particularly Bill Marsland (24th Entry), the Trenchard Librarian, and all those collaborators who in their various contributions succeeded in capturing the spirit of Halton and whose interest in their old school has kept *The Haltonian* and its predecessors flying for so many years.

The apprentices of Cranwell with their remarkable *Boys' Wing Magazine* were first in the field. Under its editor the Rev J T Skinner Law, the first Chaplain of the Boys Wing, the journal ran from Spring 1922 until the last issue, renamed *No 4 Wing Magazine,* in 1926.

The *Halton Magazine* a tri-annual journal, under the editorship of Captain A B Fanshawe AFC, MA, appeared regularly from Spring 1924 until Winter 1929. Fanshawe who became a wing commander during the war, was one of the pioneer education officers at Halton and later at Cosford until 1936. Another but shortlived Halton journal catering specifically for old Haltonians, *the Daedulus,* appeared only twice in 1927 and 1928. It was incorporated in *The Halton Magazine and the Daedulus* published from 1929 until 1935 when the title again became *The Halton Magazine,* which ran until December 1939. During the war years no magazine was issued.

In Spring 1945 publication recommenced on a biannual basis, until in 1952 it was decided to issue three numbers a year. The final number of the *The Halton Magazine* appeared in Winter 1973. A special souvenir brochure planned for Halton's Diamond Jubilee Reunion in September 1980 did not materialize. But on the basis of the articles submitted and under the editorship of Sdn Ldr Beryl Escott the *Halton Magazine,* dormant for some ten years, re-emerged in Summer 1981 under its new title *The Haltonian.* Since 1985, under editor Bill

Kelley the journal has continued to recapture memories of Halton as we knew it. My omission of honours and decorations after most names – and this throughout the book – has been solely for reasons of space! If I have overlooked someone from the following list of those who helped me with this history of No 1 School of Technical Training I can only say I am sorry:

I have to acknowledge with thanks the gracious permission of Her Majesty the Queen to reproduce the photograph of Flight Lieutenant Prince Albert RAF.

I would express my particular appreciation to:
Gp Capt G O Burton RAF, Officer Commanding RAF Halton and President of the RAF Halton Aircraft Apprentices Association, as well as its Officers and Council.
Wg Cdr C G R Greaves, CEng MRAeS RAF, formerly CTO, RAF Halton.
Flt Lt P S Brennan BA, PGCE, AMITD, RAF, RAF Cosford.
Flt Lt Ray Wittingham RAF, RAF Halton liaison officer to the Halton Aircraft Apprentices Association.
Miss Pamela Clark, Deputy Registrar and Miss Frances Dimond, Photograph Collection, The Royal Archives, Windsor.
The Royal Air Force Museum: Air Cdre D F Lawrence and Mr Peter Elliott.
Gp Capt Peter Clifford (42nd Entry).
Mr Richard Riding, Editor, *The Aeroplane Monthly*.
The Imperial War Museum, Simon Robbins and Alan Williams.
Mrs J M Buckberry, College Librarian, Royal Air Force Cranwell.
The Librarians of: The Trenchard Library RAF Halton; Royal Aeronautical Society; Bundesarchiv Militärarchiv, Freiburg, Germany; The House of Lords; Institution of Mechanical Engineers; United Nations Geneva.
Royal Air Force News.
Public Record Office.
Air Cdre Sir Frank Whittle for details concerning his apprentice days and permission to reproduce his Cranwell model-aircraft portrait.
Miss Christina Goulter, Air Historical Branch, for providing early Halton reference sources.
Ministry of Defence: information on Army Apprentices; Naval Artificers.
Wg Cdr Charles T Kimber (deceased) for personal communications.
Andrew Adam, author of *Bayonets and Beeches, The book of Halton,* for his 'Merciful Heavens . . .' piece, extracts from notes on Halton Commandants and advice.
Roger Fendley, Secretary, RAF Boy Entry Association.
Tom Oliver, Secretary, RAF Cranwell Apprentices Association.
Freddy Joyce, information on RAF Ruislip Apprentices.
Sir George Edwards.
Bob Cooper (36th Entry), J R Frapwell (38th Entry), Jack Neville (40th Entry), Aubrey Jones (40th Entry), Ron Cattell (41st Entry) MA FLCC FBIM FESB

FCollP, Norman Chell (41st Entry) PhD (Brunel), Hugh Blissett, Gerry Hatt (author of *Have spanner – will travel)*, Max Cocker, Robert Brown, Aubrey L Carter, Ron Pengelly, John Rilett – all 41st Entry. Jerry Jeremy (45th Entry), John Careless (47th Entry) author of *Trenchard's Brat*, Peter Large (57th Entry), Wg Cdr Mike Hines (63rd Entry).

I would express my appreciation also to all the subscribers whose pre-publication orders enabled publication to go ahead – I intended to include their names in an appendix but when the list topped 700 this just proved unfeasible. Last but not least, I would thank my wife Nicole for her patience in allowing me to stack most horizontal surfaces in our home with books, papers and miscellaneous Haltonia.

ORGANIZATION HALTON

This summary of organizational changes introduced at Halton from 1916 to 1941 is based on entries in the Halton Operations Record Book, miscellaneous orders, notes and personal letters.

An RFC RECRUIT TRAINING UNIT was active by the end of 1916; AUSTRALIAN FLYING CORPS TRAINING DEPOT departed on 12.6.1918.

SCHOOL OF TECHNICAL TRAINING (MEN) HALTON

Formed on 10.9.1917 under Lt Col Ian Bonham Carter, then responsible to War Office D Air O: B Section (Men) later No 4 Section existed until 15.11.1923 (Command Order 245/23), the School of TT (Men) included a Boys' Training Centre (24.9.1917).

BOYS TRAINING DEPOT HALTON
(Formed 9.10.1919)

C Section (Boys)   D Section (Boys)

NO 1 SCHOOL OF TECHNICAL TRAINING (BOYS) HOME
(as from 23.12.1919)

NO 1 SCHOOL OF TECHNICAL TRAINING (BOYS) HALTON
(as from 26.4.1920)
(and No 2 S of TT (Boys) renamed No 2 S of TT (Boys) Cranwell) both these units under DRO Part IV to DTO AM on 26.4.1920).

No 1 Section   No 2 Section   No 3 Section
NO 1 SCHOOL OF TECHNICAL TRAINING (APPRENTICES) HALTON
(Formed January 1922)

No 1 S disbanded 1.9.22; **No 2 S** Reformed as **No 2 App Wing**; **No 3 S** disbanded 27.1.23
22.10.1925 (AMWO 649/25)   (CRNO/5291/1 of 23.1.23)
No 1 S Reformed 1.4.23
(School orders 09/23)

No 1 Wing   No 2 Wing
Formed 22.10.1925

No 4 Wing
Formed August 1926
on transfer from Cranwell:
disbanded Dec 1931 to
become Administrative
Wing.

No 3 Wing
Formed 1.1.1936

No 4 Wing reformed
on 3.8.1936

As from 3 August 1936, there were four Apprentice Wings until July 1937 when **No 5 (Apprentice) Wing** formed which existed until August 1938, when it became No 5 (Airmen's) Training Wing for flight mechanics and flight riggers until March 1939.

On 31 May 1941 Apprentices in No 2 Wing transferred to **No 1 Wing** when No 2 Wing became Airmen's Training Wing.

HALTON APPRENTICES' SONG

How green are the beeches that grow on the Chilterns,
At Halton, up Beacon and Boddington crown,
But best I remember when beech leaves were falling
And painting the hillside a deep golden brown.

When beech leaves are falling, are falling, are falling
Wherever I'm stationed, where'er I may roam
Old memories come calling, come calling, come calling,
Of youth's golden scenery, of Halton and home.

(First two verses)

INTRODUCTION

Books about the Royal Air Force mostly ignore the engineers who design and construct aircraft, and particularly those who maintain them – often under conditions far different from those existing on the factory floor. The Gulf War demonstrated the rapidity of operations where aircraft readiness demands instant turnrounds. First-line servicing of operational aircraft consists of instant fault diagnosis followed by rapid component or electronic unit exchange. Anything more calls for major repair at base or by the manufacturer.

But in the past, both in war and peace, detailed inspections and repairs often had to be carried out in the desert or jungle. The workshop, if it existed, might have been under canvas or in the open, exposed to tropical or arctic weather. All this, plus the threat of air or ground attack, complicated the task of ground engineers. Servicing equipment such as overhead gantries, forklift trucks, machine and power tools, specialized test equipment, detailed repair specifications and makers' drawings were not always available even in peacetime. In these circumstances, the serviceability of an aircraft depended upon the personal initiative and training of the ground engineers. One wartime WAAF neatly summarized things when she said, someone has to put the IT in the *Spit*, the HURRY in the *Hurricane* and the IMP in the Wimpy (*Wellington*).[1]

That someone had probably been trained at Halton. It was thanks to Lord Trenchard's foresight that the vast expansion of the Royal Air Force before the last war became possible. The thorough engineering training given to apprentices, often criticized on grounds of cost, proved itself to be a wise investment. Very many ex-apprentices of all ranks qualified for rapid promotion to senior and commissioned posts during the first years of the war.

Before the end of World War I to meet the urgent need for trained ground engineers in a wide variety of trades, Trenchard conceived and planned the Royal Air Force apprenticeship scheme. In this way, the Boys' Training School, set up at Halton on 10 September 1917, produced fitters and riggers for the Royal Flying Corps. In October 1919, a similar school was formed alongside the Cadet College at Cranwell, at which the first entry of boys began their training. In March 1920, the school at Halton was renamed No 1 School of Technical Training (Boys), and that at Cranwell No 2 School of Technical Training (Boys) until April 1921 when it became Boys' Wing Cadet College Cranwell.[2]

No 1 School of Technical Training (Boys) Halton was formed on 23 December 1919. Halton received its first entry of Aircraft Apprentices in January 1922 and Apprentice training at Halton continued uninterrupted since that date until the final graduation parade of No 155 Entry on 24 June 1993.

In July 1919 'Halton Camp' was accorded Command status as an Area Command, the title changing to RAF Halton early in 1920. This continued until Training Command was formed on 1 May 1936. On 27 May 1940, Training Command divided into Flying Training Command and Technical Training Command which latter included Halton. On 1 June 1968 the two were again merged to form Training Command until 13 June 1977 when Training Command and Support Command were merged to form RAF Support Command.[3]

The Royal Air Force has in the past always depended upon Halton-trained graduates. Between January 1935 and August 1940 no less than 11,000 apprentices passed through Halton. Over the 27-years' period between 1966 to 1993, however, a total of only 3,000 apprentices completed their training. The normal intake was two entries a year except in 1941 when there was only one entry (No 43). Between 1946 and 1963 there were three entries a year and in May 1983 there was no entry (No 141) at all. Since then, apprentices have continued to arrive at No 1 School of Technical Training at the rate of two entries a year.

At the height of the Second World war over five thousand airmen were undergoing training at Halton; however, in the initial euphoria of peacetime Europe the figure declined rapidly. The three-year apprenticeship remained the core of RAF technical training, but by the mid-1950's with the onset of the 'Cold War', the number of apprentices at Halton had declined to about 2,500. In 1964, apprentice training was reorganized into Technician and Craft streams, and was expanded to include such new trades as Dental Technician. Numbers continued to decline, and in 1972 the apprenticeship was again reorganized.[4]

In peace as in war, the influence of Halton both on the ground and in the air, at all levels from technician to air marshal, has played a vital role in the achievements of the Royal Air Force. Very many ex-apprentices have become pilots or aircrew. In Fighter Command alone in the Battle of Britain, the names of 78 ex-apprentice pilots have, **so far**, been identified as having flown in those fateful days between July and October 1940. This figure will undoubtedly be greater once the records of all the fighter pilots have been reconstituted. At the beginning of the war, Wg Cdr Kimber (18th Entry) was stationed at Wattisham with *Bleinheim* day-bombers. At that time some 60% of aircrew and nearly all the technical NCO's were ex-apprentices. As Marshal of the Royal Air Force, Lord Portal, said of Trenchard's 'brats' at the end of the war, 'Their success in the air and on the ground pays a finer tribute than any words of mine to the standard of Halton's achievements.'[5]

The Victoria Cross was posthumously awarded to Sergeant Thomas Gray

(20th Entry) an Air Observer-Navigator in June 1940.

Only one of five Fairey *Battles* returned from a low-level bombing operation against bridges at Veldwezelt and Vroenhoven in the face of overwhelming odds. At least five members of the crews were ex-Brats. Gray was one of four brothers who at various times were No 1 Wing apprentices. Other distinctions to ex-apprentices include four George Crosses, 220 DFC's, 249 DFM's, more than 1,800 mentions in dispatches, and numerous other awards and decorations.[6]

From the earliest days it was Trenchard's wish that selected apprentices should go on for officer training at the Cadet College Cranwell. By 1973, the 300 ex-apprentices who had graduated from the College had been awarded 11 Swords of Honour and a total of fifty prizes. In 1993, 56 of the ex-Cranwell Cadets were still serving (see Appendix F).

In his Trenchard Memorial Lecture delivered at the Halton Branch of the Royal Aeronautical Society in April 1990, Air Chief Marshal Sir Michael Armitage (56th Entry) said that a total of some 35,000 RAF apprentices had graduated. Meanwhile, 20% of all ex-apprentices had been commissioned, and that at the present time 239 of all their engineer officers and 7.5% of serving RAF officers were ex-Apprentices. In 1986 there had been five serving ex-Apprentice Air Marshals, including the Chief of Air Staff.

It must be remembered, however, that No 1 School of Technical Training Halton has not been the only RAF apprentices' school, similar training establishments have existed at Cranwell, Flowerdown, Ruislip, Cosford, Hereford, Locking and Eastchurch – all of which have proved their worth. At Flowerdown (1922-1929) alone, of the 745 apprentices trained there, all of whom were inducted at Halton, 65% were commissioned of which nine reached air rank and more than 90 became group captains and wing commanders. Likewise, it must be remembered that RAF Halton over the years has been the home of other units, including of course the all-important Princess Mary's RAF Hospital.[7]

In the 'thirties, recruiting consisted almost entirely of short-service commissioned officers who served four years on the active list and six on the reserve. Ground staff served slightly longer terms but the backbone of the service was provided by ex-Cranwell cadets and the ex-apprentices, not forgetting the 1,770 apprentice clerks who had entered Ruislip between 1925 and 1939, prior to closure of the scheme in 1942. The reserve strength was bolstered in 1936 by the creation of the RAF Volunteer Reserve which complimented the Royal Auxiliary Air Force, or 'week-end' air force as it had become known since its inception in 1925. The Royal Air Force which in 1934 numbered only 31,000 regulars, by the time war was declared had expanded to 118,000 with a reserve force of some 45,000.[8]

But by the end of 1937, only 22 *Hurricanes* and 2 *Spitfires* could be put in the air although the expansion scheme had in 1936 provided for the construction of respectively, 1,000 and 320 of these fighters. In August 1938, when Lord

Balfour, Under-Secretary of State for Air visited the fighter station at RAF Duxford he inspected the two operational planes which he referred to as "50 per cent of the RAF front line in *Spitfires*".[9]

The expansion of the air force in the 'thirties attracted large numbers of secondary schoolboys with an interest in aviation and as a result the 33rd to 38th entries that began their Halton training between January 1936 and August 1938 numbered about 1,000 apprentices per entry. The 39th and 40th entries were slightly larger, and at the outbreak of war 4,000 apprentices were undergoing training at Halton.

The increasing size of apprentice intakes to Halton during the six-year period before the war is shown below:

YEAR	ENTRY NUMBER	ANNUAL INTAKE
1934	29th and 30th	638
1935	31st and 32nd	1,466
1936	33rd and 34th	1,934
1937	35th and 36th	2,096
1938	37th and 38th	2,135
1939	39th and 40th	2,467

then from 1940, with the 41st and 42nd Halton entries together totalling 926 apprentices, the annual war-time intakes dropped to less than 1,000 a year.

During 1940 with the arrival of the 41st Entry some of the apprentices to be trained as instrument makers or wirelesss operator mechanics transferred to Cranwell, while the fitter armourers moved to Cosford. But in August the Instrument School, including those of the 41st Entry, transferred to Halton. The fitter armourers also returned from Cosford at the beginning of 1941. On 31 May that year the remaining apprentices of No 2 Wing (which then became No 2 Airmen's Training Wing) moved over to No 1 Wing.

The concentrated training introduced for RAF apprentices in 1939, beginning with the 35th Entry that passed out six months sooner than scheduled, became even less until August 1943 when with the arrival of the 47th Entry the normal three-year period was reintroduced:

ENTRY NO											
35	36	37	38	39	40	41	42	43	44	45	46
YEARS											
2.5	2.2	2.25	1.75	1.75	1.25	2	2	2	2	2	2.5

[10]

Unlike the Army and Navy, between World War I and II there was no engineering branch in the Royal Air Force. Officers for technical duties in the RAF were seconded from the General Duties branch and received engineering training. Those officers so trained were employed alternately in technical and general duties posts. In 1932 junior technical posts were filled by a small number of commissioned warrant officers employed either on stations or maintenance units. In addition there were the 'starred' specialists drawn from those officers who had obtained an honours engineering degree before entering the GD branch.

Plans were approved in July 1939 for the setting up of a Technical Branch (subsequently the Engineer Branch). But it was April 1940 before engineer, signals and armament sections were formed; an electrical engineering section being added later. Commissioned warrant officers and qualified officers holding emergency commissions, many of whom were ex-apprentices, transferred to the new branch.[11]

Recruitment for engineer posts continued to rely extensively on ex-apprentice applicants selected mainly from personnel stationed in the United Kingdom. In 1941, 250 ex-apprentices were selected to attend a six-months' engineering course at various universities and colleges. On completion of this 'crash' course they completed the Engineering Officers' Course at Cosford.[12]

Thus by 1942 many of the engineering officers and nco's were ex-apprentices. For the RAF to have expanded to a worldwide force numbered in millions of men in the short space of less than three years, and then revert in 1945 to a peace-time pre-war role with large-scale demobilization, was nothing short of miraculous and no commercial organization could have kept going in such conditions. For their wartime performance, the contribution of apprentices was referred to by Air Chief Marshal Sir Hugh Lloyd, GBE, KCB, MC, DFC, LLD who wrote "it would have been a poor war for all of us had there not been a Halton".[13]

NOTES

Introduction

1 J Brown, *Ground Staff,* London 1943, pp 59/60
2 AMW0 9/1920 (AHB)
3 AHB, Note 41 (obtained from Unit location lists)
4 'Short History of No 1 School of Technical Training',
  brochure *Presentation of the Second Replacement Colour to No 1 School of Technical Training RAF Halton,* 1990.
5 Kimber, op cit (jacket)
6 Armitage, op cit; Kimber, op cit, pp 94,95;
  Air 8/10; 'RAF Halton' AHB5, 12.12.1956
  The Haltonian, Summer 1983 (Chaz Bowyer)
7 L L R Burch, *The Flowerdown Link* 1918-1078, 1980, p45
8 M Montgomery Hyde, British Air Policy between the Wars, London, 1976, pp 353/354; 'Apprentices and Boy Entrants by years 1919-39' prepared by M Stats 1951 for AHB 5 (Sept 1955)

22

 ‌‌

9 Montgomery Hyde, op cit, p 427
10 Kimber, op cit, pp 88/89, 376
11 AM Pamphlet 209: *The history, organization and channels of working of the RAF Technical Branch*, May 1948
12 *The Haltonian*, Summer 1986
13 Kimber, op cit, pxxi;
Andrew Boyle, *Trenchard*, 1962;
Montgomery Hyde, *op cit.*

Chapter One

FATHER OF THE ROYAL AIR FORCE

It is thanks to the 'Father of the Royal Air Force', a title Lord Trenchard hated, that an independent air force gained air supremacy and hence victory in the Battle of Britain. Equally, it is entirely due to Trenchard's foresight that Halton and Cranwell were formed at an early stage to train the leaders of an air force that by 1942 had mushroomed into a worldwide force.

In 1927 he was promoted Marshal of the Royal Air Force and in this capacity frequently attended passing-out parades at Halton. On the occasion of the 25th anniversary of Halton in 1945, he said that Halton training was the finest in the country and that the Halton spirit was the backbone of the maintenance of the RAF. At the passing out parade of the 57th Entry in 1950 he said 'Halton and Cranwell are the two pillars on which the RAF is maintained. Show by your pride and keeness that education here is worth coming to for the value in your future lives. Life is made up of unfairness; rise above it and do your best to leave your job better than you found it'.[1]

Trenchard, who had failed the entrance examination for Sandhurst, entered the Army through the militia. He was 40 when he qualified as a pilot with the Royal Flying Corps in 1912, and three years later took over command of the Royal Flying Corps France from General Henderson. Trenchard said to one officer reporting to him 'Whatever you might have heard to the contrary, I am not so bad a person to serve under' – it was generally agreed that this was so.[2]

Following acceptance of the visionary *Smuts Report on Air Organization* – with its insistence on one unified Air Service – the first problem Trenchard resolved on becoming Chief of Air Staff early in 1918, was the amalgamation of the RFC and RNAS to form the Royal Air Force on 1 April 1918. Trenchard's resignation after only a few months in office was followed in March 1919 by his reappointment as CAS, which appointment he held until his 'retirement' from the active list ten years later when he became a peer of the realm.

The battle on whether control of the new arm should be in the hands of the army or navy was won by Trenchard's insistence on having an independent air force. His detailed Memorandum for the permanent organization of the Royal

Air Force, issued as a White Paper (*CMD* 467) in December 1919, was presented to parliament by Churchill, then Secretary of State for Air. The first priority was eliminating flying accidents which in a highly technical service would be done by training boys entered on the basis of a competitive examination for a three-year apprenticeship. To replace the skilled mechanics that had been lost [by 1920, 227,000 airmen had been demobilized] selected boys were to be trained first at Cranwell and later at Halton Park as soon as permanent barracks could be built. On passing their final examination, the boys would be graded as leading aircraftsmen, and a certain number specially selected for a further course of training, at the end of which they would either be granted commissions or promoted to corporal. Those granted commissions would join the cadet college.[3]

In 1919 the RAF did not possess one single permanent barracks. Despite adverse criticism, Trenchard's plan called for large capital outlay during the first few years on permanent barracks, for the apprentices at Halton and the Cadet College, rather than on personnel and equipment. Meanwhile, if the Air Force was to be more than a means of conveyance, the air force officer had not to be merely a chauffeur since technical experts were required in the developing science of aeronautics. One of Trenchard's governing principles was to provide for the needs of the moment while laying the foundations of a highly-trained and efficient force which, though not capable of expansion in its existing form, could be made so without any drastic alteration if and when the need should arise. As a result the Fascist threat to peace in the late 1930's found the Royal Air Force geared for rapid expansion.[4]

Trenchard's announced retirement in 1929 as Chief of Air Staff was the subject of an editorial in *Flight*:

'Such an event will mark the end of an epoch, for it is Sir Hugh Trenchard who has laid the foundation stone of the first air force in the history of the world, and has been building on that stone for the last nine years....Many a general has won the affection of his fighting men in the field, but has failed when seated at the desk of the administrator. Sir Hugh Trenchard did not fail. It was probably the best thing which could have happened that the enormous, ill-disciplined air force, equipped with machines most of which were obsolescent, melted away in a few months...The Chief of the Air Staff was able to keep but a few of the officers and men, and so he was free to pick only the very best...Its uniform was in a state of flux; new titles had to be invented...He was free to decide whether a pilot should normally be an officer or an airman. He had to provide for the future supply of both commissioned and other ranks....We have said that on paper Sir Hugh Trenchard had few qualifications for such a task. It should be added that at the beginning his co-adjutors were all very youthful men for the positions which they were called on to hold, and nearly all of them had more experience in the air than at the desk. Yet the work has been done, and it has, beyond question been well done. The Royal Air Force is still small, but it is growing. Its flying efficiency is admittedly the best of any air service in the world. Both Cranwell and Halton turn out each year a class of officer and airman of just the right type for the service . . . Looked at broadly, the work of Sir Hugh Trenchard has been good, and he has gloriously stultified by his later career the decisions of the Sandhurst examiners thirty years ago.'[5]

T E Lawrence who had a very high opinion of Trenchard, said of him, '. . . He knows; and by virtue of this pole-star of knowledge he steers through all the ingenuity and cleverness and hesitations of the little men who help or hinder him'. As a staff officer, however, Trenchard was far from being perfect. His mind worked quicker than his tongue with the result that when he expressed himself on paper the result was far from what he intended. Trenchard once said to his Personal Assistant 'I can't write what I mean, I can't say what I mean, but I expect you to know what I mean'.[6]

According to Marshal of the Royal Air Force Sir John Slessor, his instructions were often a cause of puzzlement – and sometimes amusement – to his staff . . . but he had the gift of getting at the really essential core of a problem.[7]

As a pilot his flying left much to be desired, and at the prize-giving ceremony on the graduation of the 10th apprentice entry in December 1927, Trenchard confided that he was the worst pilot in the RAF. That same day he had flown to Halton in a World War I Bristol *Fighter* and landed safely only after several attempts.[8]

Towards the end of the war in the House of Lords, Trenchard spoke at length about Halton:

'Some of your Lordships will remember that after the last war we set up in the Air Force a very large training school at Halton for the men of the Royal Air Force. It was, I believe, the largest of its kind in the world. It was a great experiment and it was bitterly criticized at the time. Nevertheless, I feel justified in saying that the experiment has richly justified itself. There is no doubt at all, in my opinion, that Halton and the Halton spirit have been a pillar of strength in the Royal Air Force all over the world. The Halton-trained men have provided the nucleus on which the great expansion of the Air Force was centred. They have set and maintained an extraordinary high standard of efficiency. You have only to look at the promotions and the honours gained. Over 1,000 high honours gained, and a large number of these men are very senior Air Vice-Marshals and Air Commodores, running the highest technical offices in the Air Force (see Appendix J). Surely the efficient maintenance of aircraft has also been one of the outstanding features of this war and that has made possible by Halton training of our men.

When we originally formed the Air Force in those days we were told – and I want particularly to emphasize this because of its bearing on the future – that we were spending all our money on bricks and mortar, and on ground staff and ground personnel. In fact, some of your Lordships will remember that it was called 'the Ground Force' and I believe I was myself once described as 'GOC Ground Force'. That was because we put all the pressure we could on getting a sound foundation for training, in spite of the expense. Has this policy not justified itself ? Is it not one of the main reasons why the *Luftwaffe* has been defeated ? Did not Coastal Command show it when they went into action on the first day of the war ? The whole work of the Air Force has shown what training is doing. But there is no getting away from the fact that that it is expensive. There is nothing to show for it in peacetime, but in war-time there is just this difference to show for it – the difference between defeat and victory. Therefore I hope for the good of the Air Force to see Halton enlarged to take at least 4,000, and at least one other Halton built....The selection of the right type of boy for these schools of technical training is important. There is no danger of our not getting a sufficient number of boys in this to fill the schools . . . If the education given by the Government is as good as we gave at Halton before this war, if we can keep up that scale of education, there will be no difficulty in getting boys of the right type to join . . .' [9]

The concept of Halton had been seriously threatened in 1921 when the Geddes Committee concerned with effecting economies in government expenditure gave Lord Trenchard some sleepless nights. One of Sir Eric Geddes' proposals had been to shut down the training centre at Halton. Trenchard's arguments that a qualified Halton boy was an integral part of the RAF's specialist backbone led to Geddes, 'finally recommending that the RAF should prolong the careers of future boy technicians. Let them sign on, he urged, for two extra years . . . Trenchard eagerly complied'.[10]

In the summer of 1937, on one of Trenchard's visits to Germany, Goering gave a banquet in his honour. As the wine flowed and toasts were exchanged, Goering made it evident that they had a better impression of the RAF's spirit and training than of its size and aircraft. The evening closed with Goering escorting Trenchard into the cold night air to see the fireworks display. Goering called for a German general's greatcoat to be put around Trenchard's shoulders. The evening ended abruptly when the guests heard the amplified recording of an artillery barrage with a background of whining dive-bombers. 'That's German might for you' Goering shouted, 'I see you trembled – one day German might will make the whole world tremble'. Trenchard blazing with anger retorted, 'You must be off your head, you said earlier that you hoped we wouldn't have to fight each other.' He then added, 'I hope so too, for your sake. I warn you Goering, don't underestimate the Royal Air Force'. The aftermath came in July 1945 when accompanied by a young ex-apprentice squadron-leader they surveyed the ruined streets of Berlin. Recalling Goering's earlier boast, Trenchard said, 'He made one mistake . . . he thought too much of numbers, too little of men . . .' [11]

Trenchard's influence during his ten years as Chief of Air Staff resulted in the introduction of the short-service commission scheme, the Auxiliary Air Force, the Cadet College at Cranwell, the Staff College, and probably the most important of all the Appentice scheme. At the Halton Jubilee commemoration on 31 May 1945, in addressing the parade Lord Trenchard said to the assembled apprentices 'Nothing but the best is any good in the Air Force'.

On his resignation as Chief of the Air Staff in 1929, Trenchard remarked to a friend that he had laid the foundations of a castle, and if anyone wanted to build anything bigger than a cottage it would at any rate be a very good cottage. As a former Editor of *The Aeroplane* expressed it at the time of the Battle of Britain, the events which began in 1937 after our unhappy attempt at one-sided disarmament, had demonstrated the foresight of Lord Trenchard. To-day a castle had been built on his foundations far bigger than even he visualised when he laid them.[12]

As the system of apprenticeship dwindled in industry the concept had developed in the Air Force thanks to Trenchard. E C Shepheard, writing in 1939, said this was one of his best ideas for it combined an engineering training appropriate to the requirements of the Service with an education in the ways and traditions of the Service. It permeated the units with a mechanical aristocracy who arrived at the squadrons full of the spirit of the game . . .[13]

Sir George Edwards, a Past-President of the Royal Aeronautical Society, summed up Trenchard's influence on the Royal Air Force. In presenting the Third Trenchard Memorial Lecture at the Halton Branch of the Royal Aeronautical Society on 22 February 1960, he recalled how he had arranged for

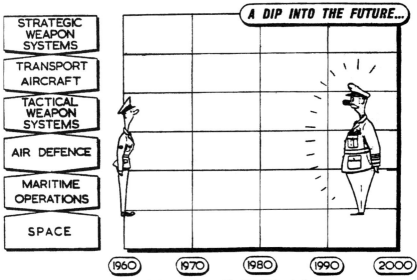

Aircraft Apprentice to Air Chief Marshal.

Trenchard to fly in the first of Britain's V Bombers, the Vickers *Valiant*. As the architect and inspiration behind the Royal Air Force, Hugh Trenchard had foreseen the strategic possibilities of Air Power by creating the first independent Air Force in the world – a step that had taken the Americans nearly 30 years to follow. Trenchard's leadership stemmed from his vision, conviction, courage, and tenacity – qualities that had to be acquired. 'Here at Halton – ' the speaker informed the apprentices, 'one of the corner stones upon which Trenchard built the Air Force – the conditions are created in which you, if you try, can acquire these qualities in some degree'. There was nothing to prevent one of the apprentices present from becoming a future Chief of Air Staff.

In a tribute to Trenchard's insistence that the future of the Air Force would depend upon the quality of the men who would serve in it, he insisted that it was not only technical qualifications which would count. He illustrated this with a story of a woman who had employed an Indian electrician to do some work in her house. Not able to explain exactly what she required, she said 'Can I leave it to your common sense?' The Indian replied, 'Madam, common sense is a rare and priceless gift of God. All I have is a technical education.'

In his lecture 'The Royal Air Force 75 Years On' delivered to the Air League in November 1993, Air Chief Marshal Sir Michael Graydon, Chief of the Air Staff, also paid tribute to Lord Trenchard's foresight. In discussing Ground Training Rationalisation, he mentioned that sadly, apprentices would no longer be trained at Halton. He emphasized that the effectiveness of the Royal Air Force still depended on loyalty, leadership, morale, ethos, tradition and the pursuit of excellence. All these qualities had been insisted upon by Trenchard to ensure that he could reconstitute the Air Force when inevitably it would be needed.[14]

NOTES

1 Father of the Royal Air Force

1 *The Haltonian*, Summer 1982
2 *Flight*, 27.12.1929
3 *ibid*, 18.12.1919
  The Times, 17.12.1919
4 *Flight*, 18.12.1919
  Montgomery Hyde, op cit, pp 73/74
5 *Flight* 27.12.1928
6 Montgomery Hyde, op cit, p 57
7 R H Fredette, *The First Battle of Britain 1917-1918*, p 253
8 *The Haltonian*, Autumn 1983 (Spencer E Viles)
9 *Hansard HL* 6.12.1944

10 Andrew Boyle, *Trenchard*, 1962, pp 404, 405
    NOTE This extension of service on the active list to twelve years, instead of ten years, from the age of 18 meant that apprentices' attested to serve beyond the maximum allowable term of twelve-years stipulated in the Army (Annual) Act, applicable to the Air Force. This was corrected in 1955 when the relevant legislation was repealed (personal letter 15.2.1990, Statutory Publications Office).
11 ibid, pp 708, 709, 730
12 C G Grey, *A History of the Air Ministry*, 1940 in *Wings of War*, 1942, p 84.
13 E C Shepheard, *The Air Force of Today*, 1939
14 ACM Sir Michael Graydon,The Humphrey Memorial Lecture 1993: The Royal Air Force 75 Years On, delivered on 6 November 1993.

Chapter Two

THE FOUNDATIONS

Royal Air Force Halton, is traversed from end to end by an old Roman road – the upper Icknield Way – connecting Wendover with Ivinghoe and Luton in its course to the East coast. The Halton estate as it was once known belonged to the Dashwood family, and the old Dashwood Manor was replaced by a Rothschild Manor known as Halton House, the present RAF Officers' Mess. Halton situated on the north-western slopes of the Chiltern Hills is an hour's train journey from London. The town of Aylesbury which is some four or five miles away is visible from the higher points of the camp. Roughly 500 feet above sea level the guide books describe the position as undoubtedly most healthy.

In his book *Beechwoods and Bayonets*, Andrew Adam recounts that the manor of Haltone mentioned in the Domesday Book of 1086 had by the 18th century become an estate of 1,500 acres with stone cottages, lanes and beechwoods. In 1853, Baron Lionel Rothschild acquired the Halton estate for £47,000 which in 1879 passed to the immensely rich and generous Alfred de Rothschild. His first creation was the lavish Halton Mansion 'an English Chateau modelled on modern French lines' built in 1883 in its magnificent setting of Halton Park. By the following year Alfred, whose guests included the Prince of Wales, shared with Queen Victoria in Buckingham Palace the distinction of being among the first in Britain to have electric lighting. The warm-air grids near the floor are still working.[1]

The first military occupation of Halton parklands dates back to 1913 when following the offer of Alfred de Rothschild, the 1st Brigade of Guards and support units, a total of 2,500 troops, participated in the Army's summer manoeuvres. Camping on the grass-covered landing field – later Maitland parade ground – were about 200 officers and airmen of No 3 Squadron of the Royal Flying Corps which had been formed on 3 May the previous year. The squadron operated with a dozen or so Bleriot monoplanes, Renault BE's and Henri Farman biplanes.

A pictorial supplement to the *Bucks Advertiser* of 27 September 1913 gave full details of Rothschild hospitality on this occasion. Plain army rations were

*An unusual photograph taken in 1919 of Sir Hugh Trenchard – the 'Father of the Royal
Air Force' – showing RAF crown and wing insignia above his AVM ranking braid.*
(Via *Aeroplane Monthly.*)

supplemented by morning coffee and biscuits, and high teas at weekends. A staff of Aylesbury caterers with numerous waiters served the delighted troops with hot pies, cold meats, chickens and hams, all washed down with tea, beer or mineral waters. Personnel of the Royal Flying Corps – the greatest attraction for the thousands of visitors – enjoyed three specially prepared meals a day served by another firm of outside caterers. Not satisfied with all this, Alfred de Rothschild supplied free cigarettes, tobacco and beer. The Officers Mess tent, adorned in gala fashion with plants and flowers from his nurseries was floodlit by paraffin lamps suspended from 40 feet high standards. Sunday visitors highly appreciated the regimental massed bands and particularly at sundown the pipes of the Black Watch. A drive round the camp by a beaming Alfred de Rothschild concluded the evening's entertainment.

Halton became an army training camp in August 1914, when Kitchener's Third New Army encamped on what was to become Halton airfield. The excellent rail and road links made Halton an ideal centre for infantry training and troop movement to France. By 1915 the camp held 5,000 troops, but at the peak of recruit training activity some 15,000 military personnel were stationed at Halton.[2]

On the death of Rothschild in January 1918 with the contents removed the house stood empty. At the determined insistence of Lord Trenchard, the estate was loaned to the War Office and later sold to the Crown.[3]

One RAF occupant some fifty years ago described the Halton Officers' Mess in extravagant terms. His wartime notes on this palatial ex-Rothschild residence leave nothing to the imagination:

'Merciful heavens! did anyone ever see so much gilt? It adorns every panel and every dome, it wreathes itself into fantastic patterns and sackbut and shawms and other musical instruments, it overflows into baskets of flowers and horns of plenty. Here it is a quiver of arrows, there it is a sprightly nymph; it runs madly along the balcony that encircles the great hall and coruscates in the railings underneath; it twines demurely in loveknots, it runs amok in palanquins and tassels or twirls itself frivously into monograms . . . There is nothing shy or retiring or modest about it. It shouts at you like the sons of God and a good deal louder.'

Andrew Adam supplements the young officer's poetical prose with a note that the *AR* monograms extended even to some of the lavatory seats.[4]

The magnificence of this converted mansion vividly contrasted with the rugged red-brick Bulbeck [Bulback] Barracks, so called from their proximity to a copse known as Bulbeck Covert. Completed in 1924, the sixteen blocks of buildings designed to accommodate 2,000 apprentices in Nos 1 and 2 Wings, no longer house twenty-two beds in their ninety-six dormitories. Transformed and converted into smaller units, the buildings together with the sergeants' messes and headquarters block, have withstood the ravages of time and generations of youthful occupation.

By 1928, Halton consisted of Bulbeck, now renamed Henderson (No 1 Wing Barracks) and Groves (No 2 Wing Barracks), together with the newer Maitland and Shepherd Barracks. In December 1931, following the economic cuts, No 4 Wing was transferred to Nos 1 and 2 Wing, and the following year No 4 Wing – which from March 1933 until November 1935 accommodated ex-apprentices attending the conversion course for training on either engines or airframes – reverted to its original title of Administrative Wing. On 1 January 1936 No 4 (Apprentices) Wing again reappeared to house the additional apprentices recruited under the RAF expansion scheme. It was not until 1936 that a No 3 (Apprentices) Wing made its appearance within Paine Barracks. This was followed in July 1937 by an additional No 5 Wing which, originally intended to house apprentices, became No 5 (Airmen) Wing.

In February 1924, a detailed description of Nos 1 and 2 Wings illustated with maps, diagrams and photographs, even down to the water pipe runs and central heating installation of the barracks appeared in three successive issues of *The Engineer*. A total of 1,352 apprentices were being trained; as fitters (including Fitters A-E, drivers petrol, or armourers) 890; carpenters (including carpenter-riggers and a small number of motor-body builders) 327; copper-smiths 35; and turners 100. This figure had, it was reported, subsequently been increased to a total of 1,950 apprentices, presumably by the new entry.

The report mentioned that 350 educational authorities had already nominated boys for the competitive entrances examinations. It referred to the selection of certain leading apprentices for cadetships at Cranwell and those nominated for an advanced course for direct promotion to corporal. There was also a reasonable opportunity for ex-apprentices to be selected for flying training and to become airmen pilots.

Entries were received in February and September, the boys being attested in the Royal Air Force for three years as aircraft apprentices and engaged 'to serve *ten* years from the age of 18, and *two* years reserve service afterwards.

School instruction at the hands of university trained staff included mathematics with differential and integral calculus for the more advanced students, properties of materials, energy, heat and electricity, with English and general studies. other subjects taught included revision of measuring instruments, machine drawing, technical writing, theory of engines and aeroplanes. It appears that the initial pay of 1s 6d a day, and 3 shillings at the age of 18, had by the 'thirties been reduced!

The dormitories, 66 feet in length, 20 feet wide and 10 feet high, had six windows in each side and one window at one end – never to be peered through if a parade was in progress! There were two rows of hot-water pipes, and for each floor of two dormitories 'there were assigned one enamelled bath, two separate shower baths, both furnished with hot and cold water, and eight wash-hand basins'. The report does not explain why the supply of water whose heating was controlled by recording thermometers in the outgoing and incoming pipes never arrived hot at the taps. The four water-closets having 'wood cleats taking the place of the more usual lifting seats' were supplemented by two 'glazed fire-clay urinals'. Undoubtedly the cleats were designed to withstand the abrasive force of a 10-inch scrubbing brush! The sanitary arrangements included on each floor of the block 'a highly appreciated' (particularly by generations of unauthorized smokers) heated fan-ventilated chamber where wet clothes could be rapidly dried.

The Halton school for technical training in 1924 (supplemented by the apprentice schools at Cranwell and Flowerdown) was described as a miniature engineering works equipped with all the machinery necessary for maintaining aircraft of all kinds. The report underlined the excellent relationship between instructors and pupils. The canteens contained recreation rooms with billiard tables and libraries where in addition to works of fiction several books dealing with 'the differential and integral calculus had evidently been handled.'[5]

NOTES

2   The foundations

1   'Halton House' (Take-away leaflet)
2   *The Haltonian,* Summer 1981
3   Grace Haydock, *Halton House*
4   Adam, op cit, p 38
     Note – None of the present lavatory seats bear the Rothschild monogram.
5   *The Engineer*, 1, 8, and 15 Feb 1924

Chapter Three

BOYS' WING ROYAL FLYING CORPS (1917-1918)

On 1 April – a recurring date in Air Force history – 1911, Britain's first Air Battalion of the Royal Engineers was formed under Major Sir Alexander Bannerman. It comprized No 1 Company at Farnborough dealing with airships and No 2 Company at Larkhill with aeroplanes.[1] That same year the Admiralty commissioned the ill-fated airship, ironically named the *Mayfly*, which was wrecked in a storm. This name was taken over in the 1920's for a small aircraft constructed by Halton Apprentices and which is described in Appendix E.

The RE Air Battalion functioned for only one year until on 3 May 1912, by Royal Warrant, it was absorbed into the Royal Flying Corps. The air service traditions of Halton go back to that period when the RFC comprized a Naval Wing (which on 23 June 1914 became the Royal Naval Air Service) a Military Wing and the Central Flying School, virtually separate branches until the formation of the Royal Air Force on 1 April 1918.[2]

Prior to the outbreak of war in 1914 the technical training of men was carried out at the Central Flying School at Netheravon where there were 200 trainees. But with the demand for specialized training, a school of instruction at Reading for 1,000 men trained riggers and fitters for the 'birdcage' type aircraft then operating in the Royal Flying Corps. From July 1916 a converted jam factory at nearby Coley was set up with 2,000 trainees. Despite these measures the number of fully trained mechanics being turned out proved inadequate for the 57 newly formed RFC squadrons.[3]

The idea of recruiting boys for the RFC was probably contained in a letter from a Colonel Wynard, Headmaster of the Gordon Boys' School, written to the War Office on 14 November 1916.

He pointed out that numbers of boys employed particularly in the munitions industry could be trained in the Army. Although at that time there were already about 100 boys serving in the RFC, Wynard's proposal was taken up and on 27 April 1917 it was decided that a scheme should be started in the RFC with an initial intake of 500 boys. When in July 1917 the War Office decided to double the number of operational squadrons to 200 some of the RFC boys were posted to units after as little as eight weeks' training.[4]

In line with the urgent need for skilled mechanics, facililties were centralized at the Halton Park estate and in July 1917 it was decided to move the School of Technical Training (Men) there from Reading. From August 1917 the soldiers were replaced by Royal Flying Corps air mechanics and administrative staff. This followed proposals made that June by General Sefton Brancker, Deputy Director-General of Military Aeronautics to coordinate the technical training of men, women and boys. The School of Technical Training (Men) was duly established at Halton on 10 September 1917, which included a Boys' Training Depot renamed in 1918 School of Technical Training (Boys). By January 1918 it came under the Army Eastern Command but still under the direct control of the War Office (D Air O). It was stipulated by a Colonel Drew that the Company officers of the Boys' Section should be education officers since their duties, besides drill and discipline, would include elementary instruction on engines, rigging, stores, etc, which an ordinary regimental officer could not undertake.[5]

When the RFC had begun recruiting for a boys' service it was merely following a long naval and military tradition. Whether as midshipmen, like Nelson who served on HMS *Raisonnable* at the age of 12, or as boy seamen, the Royal Navy had always followed a policy of catching them young. Between 1756 and 1815 some 31,000 young boys had passed into the fleet. Some of them, taken in by the Marine Society as waifs and strays, served at sea as servants and apprentices. Founded in 1905, thousands of the nation's youths were trained at Shotley in HMS *Ganges*. The fifteen months' training course for 2,000 boys aged between 15 and 16 combined seamanship and general education. This like the Naval Engine-room Artificer entrants, whose recruitment was subject as in the RAF to a stringent entry examination, proved a valuable basis for the Navy's recruitment system. These ERA's were, as one author describes them, always intended to be a small *corps d'élite*, and so they still consider themselves. Meanwhile, in the British Army boys saw active service in South Africa during the Boer War.[6]

The account by John Ross confirms the date 20 June 1917 for the arrival at Halton of the first entry of 400 in the Boys' Section of the Royal Flying Corps School of Technical Training. The boys had enlisted earlier that month at the RFC Depot, Farnborough, where after being issued with uniforms and kit they did their initial square-bashing

At West Camp Halton, depending on their heights, the boys were assigned to either 'A' or 'B' Company; in this way, Ross as a tall boy found himself in 'A' Company. Each of the four companies (each divided into Nos 1-4 Platoons) of Nos 1 and 2 Battalions, was under the command of an army Lieutenant assisted by an RFC subaltern. The Commandant Boys' Training Centre, Halton Camp West, in September that year, was Captain H L Nixon RFC. He wore an observer's badge and attended parades on horseback. Beds in the Army-type wooden huts consisted of three boards reposing on two eight-inch high trestles. Calico palliases and pillows were filled by the boys from heaps of straw in the old horse lines. Although the huts were scrubbed out weekly there were so many 'earwigs' that the boys learned to live with them. The flight-sergeants wore a four-bladed propellor – the origin of the distinguishing apprentice-wheel – above their three stripes. As well as morning and afternoon drills, the boys mounted a guard at Headquarters and at the camp entrance on the Wendover-Tring road.

Although known as the School of Technical Training, in the absence of any aircraft or tools no technical instruction was possible. After several months at Halton, following interview by their commanding officer the boys were classified as fitter-aero or rigger. Officers of the Army Education Corps in their six and sometimes three hours of instruction each week prepared them for the 2nd Class Military Certificate of Education. The programmes of school work, physical training, and 'work' were issued as typed instructions. In this way the Programme of Work dated 22 September 1917 read:

1. Lines will be inspected by the Commandant daily at 10.15 a.m.
2. Canes [longer than the later RAF crested type] will be carried three times a week and saluting drill practiced each day.
3. Lectures will be given each day on various administrative subjects including value of discipline, methods of making applications *and complaints* [Author's italics], nature of military punishment . . .

The Programme also stipulated that 'great-coats will not be worn unless orders to that effect are given by the Commandant'. Under the heading of school work, Saturday mornings were set aside for the testing of new boys.[7]

In December 1917 selected volunteers could remuster as wireless operators for posting to Farnborough, others as carpenters, transport or gunnery duties, instrument repairers or clerks.[8]

Besides the 2,000 boy mechanics at West Camp, the RFC units at Halton, under the overall command of Lt Col Ian Bonham-Carter (see Chapter 6) in 1917 included 6,000 air mechanics, 1,700 instructors and permanent staff, and last but not least some 2,000 airwomen trainees. Also at Halton was a training depot in East Camp for the Australian Flying Corps which by the end of 1918 had trained 1,200 air mechanics.[9]

The Australians received instruction on *SE 5, SE 5a, RE 8, BE 2b, FE 2b* aircraft as well as the big twin-engined Handley-Page *0/400*. Another Boy Mechanic recounts that after first kitting out at Aldershot, like Ross, in the much-admired khaki double-breasted 'maternity jackets' and breeches, he arrived at Halton in December 1917. Following intitial training on the parade ground in May 1918 he was sent to the Royal Naval Station at Cranwell for technical training.[10]

The number of boys at Halton must have increased fairly rapidly because in his letter of 4 February 1918 to the Director General of Military Aeronautics, Bonham-Carter referred to a total of 3,478 boys under training at the School of Technical Training.[11]

A Boys' Training Depot was formed at Letchworth in about June 1918, but by January the following year this unit as well as the Eastchurch Boys' Training were proposed to be disbanded.[12]

Meanwhile, conditions remained tough at Halton, the straw-filled palliases and wooden bed-boards almost at ground level were still in use. Bucket-type latrines, often frozen, housed in corrugated-iron buildings with open walls ensured adequate ventilation. Boys washed in pails of cold water or shared a communal bucket previously heated on the slow-combustion stove in their hut.

Whitewash was lavishly applied throughout the camp. In the severe winter of 1917-18 when the paths between huts became muddy tracks the wooden floors of the billets, wet-scrubbed weekly, were always damp. Food was grim even in wartime; occasionally when rations were in short supply, for their meal boys received four 'one-inch cubes' cut from a loaf of bread.

Epidemics of various diseases including diptheria, smallpox and impetigo became so rife that in January 1918 the whole camp was placed in total isolation. A distinguishing coloured tab on the boys' tunics denoted the particular disease from which they suffered: red for scarlet fever; blue for measles; white for mumps, etc. Depending on the disease, boys were assigned to squads – most dreaded was the impetigo squad where faces, ears and scalps presented some sorry sights.[13]

Sometimes squads would be marched to a building prepared as a fumigation centre. With the doors closed the fumigator would be operated and the boys called on to sing. These conditions continued until April when some boys moved into bell tents, but the first morning they woke to find the canvas bulging inwards under the weight of the snow. As they marched out of West Camp on transfer in May 1918 to Cranwell, the boys hoped they would would never see Halton again.[14]

RNAS, RFC and RAF at Cranwell (1918).

Cranwell at that time was divided into two areas: West Camp for personnel of the Royal Naval Air Service and the recently constructed East Camp for the Womens Auxilliary Air Force and the Boys' Wing. Links with the Royal Navy had dated back to the autumn of 1915. The Admiralty had then commandeered some 3,000 acres of farmland from the the the Earl of Bristol's estate for HMS *Daedulus*, the name chosen for the new Royal Naval Air Service school.[15]

For boy seamen in the Royal Navy earlier this century, discipline had been undoubtedly severe. A.E.Chambers, room orderly in T.E.Lawrence's hut at RAF Farnborough in 1922, in a recorded interview told me that he had been frequently beaten by petty officers during his Royal Navy boys' training. In reply to my question, he said 'It must have hurt, because the cane was applied over stretched, wet canvas-slacks, this while handcuffed to a table top'.

Boys at Cranwell trained either on aero engines or the fabric-covered wire-braced wooden airframes. Egles found the centrally-heated dormitories, brick-built dining halls and tarmac roads at Cranwell palatial after his experiences at Halton. With the constitution of the Royal Air Force on 1 April 1918 the RNAS and RFC were combined, the boys being given the option of continuing their service in the RAF or taking their discharge. Officers and nco's were loath to abandon their previous ranks. Whether petty officer for corporal, or flight commander and captain for flight lieutenant, the mix of khaki and navy blue adorned with fouled anchors, pips and rings was a constant source of confusion.

Flight Lieutenant HRH Prince Albert (George VI) at RAF Cranwell in April 1918 as Officer in charge of Boys' Wing. A Naval CPO surveys the variety of Boys' uniforms including one RFC "maternity jacket".
(Windsor Castle, Royal Archives,© 1992. Her Majesty the Queen.)

One of the first problems following the amalgamation of the naval and military air services was the question of terminology. Traditional naval expressions included such terms as 'ship's company', 'watches', 'aye 'aye Sir, and even the 'liberty boat' for men 'going ashore' from HMS *Daedulus* the name for the camp. These were gradually replaced so that the 'ward-room mess' became the 'officers' mess' and 'mess-deck' the 'dining room'. The 'galley' emerged as 'cookhouse', 'victuals' as 'rations', 'gear' as 'kit'. One concession was made to the sailors, according to an Air Ministry Order issued in July 1918 the use of 'port' and 'starboard' was to continue for 'left' and 'right'. On the other hand, some new terms replaced both army and naval usage: the military 'other ranks' and naval 'ratings' were replaced by the already-established term 'airmen'. As the author of *The War in the Air*, perhaps with a sly dig at high ranking 'wingless wonders' put it: 'names are full of compliment and fantasy: 'airman' is the official name for those members of the air force who spend their time and do their work on the ground'.[16]

Meanwhile, John Ross on arriving at Cranwell on 6 April 1918, found the food better than that at Halton but did not like the 'bull', a mix of mostly Navy and also Army discipline. The boys resented the order 'scrub decks' and having to roll their trousers above the knees. Technical training under naval mechanics included filing and fitting together pieces of steel followed by training in the use of scrapers on engine bearings. Then followed instruction on several aero-engines, including rotary and radial types. On reaching the age of 18 the boys were posted for on-the-job training to different Air Force units. In this way Ross completed his training at Cranwell on 28 January 1919.[17]

The future King George VI, then HRH Prince Albert on transfer from the Royal Naval Air Service, served at Cranwell from February until August 1918. The Prince's appointment, initially Officer in Charge of Boys, later became OC No 4 Squadron, West Camp. The Prince, who with the formation of the Royal Air Force on 1 April was promoted Flight Lieutenant, performed all the duties of a regular officer. Shortly after his arrival at Cranwell he was visited by the King and Queen who inspected the boys, the various machines and also the airships in their hangars.

Writing to his father on 9 February, the Prince told him that life at Cranwell was very different from that on a ship. He was in charge of 500 boys and wrote 'I shall have to punish them myself and grant their requests for leave etc . . . They live in small huts, 20 boys in each and these give me the most trouble as they won't keep them clean without my constantly telling them off to clean them out of working hours. The petty officers are not altogether satisfactory. One finds a tremendous difference between them and the proper Naval P.O. But with a little persuasion I hope to make them understand what I want'.

Prince Albert was not happy about the muddle resulting from the amalgamation of the RNAS and the RFC or with the mixture of naval and military routine. He left Cranwell for the RAF Headquarters at St.Leonard's-on-Sea on 1 August 1918 and one year later was promoted Squadron Leader.[18]

Concerning Prince Albert's routine duties, not long after my arrival at Halton in 1937 I was told an amusing, but probably apochryphal, story about his stay at

Cranwell. At that time the prince had a somewhat pronounced stutter, which it seems he later managed to overcome. Following a charge of absence without leave, one boy mechanic was overjoyed to hear: 'For . . . for . . . for . . . Seven days confined to camp'. John Ross recalls that when Prince Albert took charges against defaulters in the orderly room of the Boys' Wing he had difficulty in announcing the punishment because of this stammer.[19]

Air Mechanic Egles was still under training in November 1918 when the armistice was signed. While the airmen, headed by the station band, marched round West Camp the boys had to attend classes as usual. At tea-break that afternoon they formed up in column of fours and with one hand on the shoulder of the boy in front they marched to East Camp and to their dormitories. They ignored their commanding officer's raised hand for them to stop and before breaking up gave a resounding cheer. The next morning on parade they were informed that as they had done nothing to win the war they had no right to join in the jolifications! [20]

Halton Sports, September 1917. Lt Col Ian Bonham-Carter (right) Commandant Technical Training Halton with the officer commanding Boys' Training Centre West Camp, Captain H L Nixon RFC, who later succeeded him. Air Cdre Bonham-Carter was AOC Halton 1928-1931.

(Private Collection.)

NOTES

3 Boys' Wing Royal Flying Corps (1917-1918)

1   *Army Order* 28.2.1911
2   Clarence Winchester, *The King's Air Force*, 1937
    ABC of the RAF, 1941, p5
3   Armitage, op cit
4   ibid, op cit
5   AO/572 W.O.letter 24.9.1917/ Minute 8 30.8.1917. Adam, op cit,
    pp 91,92; Walter Raleigh, *The War in the Air*, Oxford, 1922, Vol v, p 435;
    AHB Note No 41
6   John James, *The Paladins*, London, 1990; M Lewis, *The Navy of
    Britain*, London, 1948; Armitage, op cit
    NOTE The Army Training Organization in 1993 was undergoing a major
    review (Personal letter M of D: Headquarters Doctrine and Training,
    8.9.1993). The first Army Boys' Technical School set up in 1923 at
    Aldershot moved in 1924 to Chepstowe, where in 1966 it became the
    Army Apprentices College. Up to 700 technician and craft apprentices
    were trained per annum; the two-year course trained them for the Royal
    Engineers and Royal Corps of Transport (marine engineers). Apprentices
    since 1939 have trained at the Army Technical School at Arborfield (Army
    Apprentices School from 1947), and from 1955 the College has provided
    tradesmen solely for REME with young women entrants admitted since
    May 1993. The Army Apprentices School Harrogate (960 apprentices)
    established in 1947, prepares entrants for the Royal Artillery, Royal
    Engineers, and Royal Signals (telecommunications).
7   AHB (copies of Work Programmes) '58'
8   Ross, op cit
9   Adams, op cit, p 93
10 RAF Museum (Egles)
11 Air 2/77 B545
12 AHB Note '64'
13 Armitage, op cit
14 Egles, op cit
15 *Fifty Years' of Cranwell* (1920-1970)
16 Walter Raleigh, *The War in the Air*, Oxford, 1922, vol 1, pp 210,211.
17 Ross, op cit, 119,120,136,153
18 Haslam, op cit, pp 13-17
19 Ross, op cit, pp 120-121
20 Egles, op cit

Chapter Four

EARLY DAYS HALTON/CRANWELL (1919-1926)

In June 1919, the Deputy Director of Training in the newly created Royal Air Force, a Colonel – who by the beginning of World War II had become Air Chief Marshal Sir Edgar Ludlow-Hewitt AOC-in-C Bomber Command – submitted proposals for Boys' Training. He had been instructed by Trenchard, a lifelong friend, to draft training schemes for the Secretary of State relating to officers, boy mechanics and aircraftmen. Although a decision by a Committee appointed by the War Cabinet for the question of the boys' pay was still awaited, Ludlow-Hewitt's proposals covering the general policy of education, training and examination of boy mechanics were all accepted by the Director of Training.

For the two entries a year in February and September, admission would be by competitive examination under the Civil Service Commission and a system of direct entry for those deemed educationally qualified by the Local Education Authority. Special arrangements were made for ex-service candidates who were either the sons of officers or of *technical* [Author's italics] senior NCO's. One surprizing proposal was that those selected for NCO boy ranks should receive the pay of an LAC – the Director had scored out 'AC2'– roughly four times that of a boy mechanic. Those, on the other hand, who made insufficient progress were to be discharged from the RAF – a condition which presumably was not followed for very long! A number not exceeding 5% ('2%' had been deleted) of the boys recommended at the conclusion of their training for a further six months' course of instruction would be promoted corporal. From this latter category 'a few would be selected for training as *flying* officers [Author's italics] . . . at the Cadet College'.

This mention of 'the Cadet College' – which had been inserted by Ludlow-Hewitt to replace the words 'a special school' – is of particular interest since it is probably the earliest official reference to the RAF Cadet College as such. In fact, Gp Capt Haslam' in his history of Cranwell, confirms that it was not until 2 October 1919 that Trenchard was informed of the Treasury go-ahead for the RAF Cadet College, which was opened on 5 February 1920.

The Director's comments three days later included: 'As regards numbers

CAS [Trenchard] has agreed to the entry of 2,000 boys in 1920 and 2,000 in 1921. Further expansion to be considered next year'. The immediate step was to obtain approval for the conditions of entry and age limits and to issue a statement accordingly to the Press. The final comment reads 'You must be prepared to make out a strong case for 3 years' training'.

The proposed establishments at about this time for the training of boys were:

	Boys	Officers	Other ranks
Halton Camp	3,000	35	500
Cranwell Camp	2,000	25	340
Eastchurch*	1,000	20	250
*Closed in March 1920			1

The subsequent announcement, under the heading 'Boy Mechanics in the RAF', duly appeared in *The Times* on 18 November 1919. This confirmed that boys aged 15 and 16 resident within the area of the London County Council could enlist in the RAF and 'on attaining the age of 18 they must undertake to serve in the RAF for a further period of eight years, on completion of which they will pass into the reserve for four years'.

Only two days later, however, a half-page announcement in *Flight* referred to a new scheme of entry by competitive examination for well-educated boys to train as Boy Mechanics. The age of entry was the same but the terms of service had now been extended to *ten* years' colour service followed by *two* years in the Reserve. Successful candidates would enter the training centre in February 1920. A certain number would be chosen for a further six months higher instruction 'for promotion at once to corporal'. It was explained that the scheme constituted an entire departure from the methods imposed by war conditions when boys had received only a few months' training. Entry would now be confined 'to boys of sufficient intellectual attainments to ensure that they would benefit by a long apprenticeship . . . ' [2]

Discontent over the primitive conditions still existing at Halton including poor food and accommodation finally errupted in East Camp, which housed the original RAF Boys' Section. In November 1919, armed with their rifles and bayonets, the boys from West Camp were ordered to report there to put down the disturbances which had resulted in the cookhouse and stores building being set on fire. In fact, according to one eyewitness the boys managed to dodge this duty by hiding.[3]

Meanwhile in December 1919, Winston Churchill (Secretary of State for War and Air since 14 January that year) in the debate on the *Air Estimates*, said 'with regard to Halton Park, that had been purchased by the Government . . . it was proposed to put in the grounds the principal training college for young air mechanics. There had been for a good many months between 3,000 and 4,000 boys there. The Government was going to replace the huts there on a regular system, by proper brick buildings, and make it a permanent centre for Air Force mechanical training.' [4] In his note to the Secretary of State for Air, Ludlow-Hewitt (mentioned above) had proposed that the boys should be given opportunities for taking recognized engineering examinations since the certificates obtained would prove invaluable later on.[5]

The immediate objective shown in the Appendix to *AO Memo* No 1338 (21.6.1919) was to have 3,000 boys under training on a three-year course. An Air Council memo to the Treasury said that the three-year training period proposed was shorter than that of boy recruits for the Navy. The annual intake envisaged by the Air Council was 1,500 – 2,200 boys which would provide for a force of from 28,000 to 41,000. It therefore proposed to build in the first instance for 4,000 boys. Pending completion of the barracks, the boys would be trained at Cranwell although the accommodation there could only take about 1,700 boys. Of the £1 million allocated for building work at Halton more than a half would be for the boys' accommodation.[6]

The Boys' Training Depot was formed on 9 October, but only three months later on 23 December 1919 it became the School of Technical Training (Boys), Halton. In March 1920 the name was again changed to No 1 School of Technical Training (Boys) Halton.[7]

In July 1919 the 'boys', distinguished by the four-bladed propellor below their red shoulder badges, had been issued with the Royal Air Force blue uniform.[8]

Discipline among the post-war boy trainees at Halton remained a problem. A report on an Air Ministry file summarizes complaints by The Commandant, Air Vice-Marshal F R Scarlett, (an ex-Dartmouth Cadet) on 3 January 1920 to the Department of the Director of Personnel that 'technical knowledge is crammed into the boys during all the hours of daylight, producing knowledge perhaps but without any ballast, the boys becoming undesirable members of the RAF and liable to be insubordinate at the least provocation'. In his view the NCO's, who were of poor quality since the best had left the service, should be replaced by 'very specially efficient NCO's . . . to carry the boys through their 18 months' training and look after not only the boy's discipline but also his general welfare, including his cleanliness, manners, and domestic affairs, as is the custom in the Navy, with most beneficial results'.

The Air Commodore emphasized the scattered and open nature of Halton Camp and the fact that a new camp with proper enclosure was to be built. He felt that leave should not be given to boys without their parents' consent and that the first six months of training should concentrate on drill, discipline and education. He also considered that the recruiting officers should be more selective in the first instance which did not appear to be the case.

The upshot was that a fenced 'special confinement camp' was set up for defaulters. Restrictions included: absolute silence except for ten minutes after meals during which they would be seated at two-yard intervals; all marching and orders to be obeyed at the double. Only books of an instructional nature were to be taken into a special reading and writing hut where all boys would be required, under supervision, to write home twice weekly. Apart from a fifteen minute period before Roll Call in the evening complete silence was to be maintained. A frequently recurring theme in the boys' letters would certainly have been 'spent a quiet day'!

Although a Court Martial or Detention was deemed to be undesirable for boy offenders, serious offences would be dealt with by the civil power while repetition of serious military offences would be dealt with by dismissal from the RAF. Col Ludlow-Hewitt, now signing as a Group Captain, endorsed the previous recommendations on the Air Ministry file to the effect that the boys had completed 12 months' training but still had another 12 months to go. He considered that 'Restriction of privileges' rather than severe measures should prove effective but preferred to have the opinion of Air Commodore Scarlett, the AOC Halton. In March 1920, an amendment to *King's Regulations for the RAF* contained the following passages:

> 'Boys, even more than men, require handling with tact and sympathy. Discipline must be taught and maintained, but discipline based only on fear of punishment is of little value, and cannot be relied upon in emergencies or when close supervision is impossible. Officers and NCO's should take pains to interest themselves in the boys as individuals, and endeavour to win their confidence . . . They should spare no pains in providing and organising amusements and occupations for all leisure hours . . .'

The opening ceremony of the original single-bay building of the 'New Workshops' had been performed by Trenchard in 1918. By mid-1920 the Workshops were under the control of a Captain and an RSM both from the Guards – two of the smartest men in the Army at that time. The Guardroom was a corrugated iron building against the Parade Ground with a clock facing the square. On one occasion the RSM threatened one boy by saying, 'You see that clock, well, on the other side of that wall you can hear it tick!' Boy Mechanics marched down the hill to workshops headed by the Bugle Band. Outstanding trainees were made 'Senior Boys' – distinguished by 'green cords' worn round their left shoulder.[9] Following a proposal by the Camp Commandant to Air Ministry, distinctive coloured capbands were issued in September 1920 to indicate in which of the Sections the 4,000 boys belonged. This was to facilitate identification in the workshops or Regimental Institute or in cases 'such as trespass outside the Camp'. He had decided not to proceed with the suggestion of having two coloured triangles sewn on the back of each boy's tunic owing to the amount of tailoring involved ![10]

Under Lord Trenchard's scheme, the first entry of 235 Boy Mechanics in February 1920 had been sent to Cranwell with another 242 boys in September,

40 specially selected entrants from each intake being sent on to Flowerdown for training in the new skill of of Wireless Operator Mechanic. In March it was designated No 2 School of Technical Training (Boys) Cranwell until in April 1921 it reverted to 'Boys Wing' Cadet College, Cranwell. This was once again changed to No 4 (Apprentices) Wing in October 1925 when it was transferred to Halton (see below).[11]

Meanwhile, under the title 'RAF Vacancies for RAF Mechanics', *The Times* gave details of an open competition to fill 300 vacancies for candidates who would enter in January 1921. A pamphlet giving particulars of training and systems of entry was also mentioned. The announcement was repeated in August the following year by which time the age limits were given as 15 to 16½, as at 1 January 1922.[12]

Boy Mechanic Walter Dawson who arrived at Halton in 1919 replied to an advertisement for Cranwell Cadets. After passing the examination he completed officer training at the College. Not only was he the first Halton boy to obtain a cadetship but he retired from the RAF as Air Chief Marshal.

In September 1921, *the Editor of Flight* reported that a contingent of some 500 boys had just left King's Cross for Cranwell, their destination was given as the 'R.A.F. School for Technical Training for Boys'.

Enter the Aircraft Apprentices

The following month *Flight* reviewed Sir Ian Hamilton's book, *The Soul and Body of an Army*. In speaking of future warfare, the author had said 'We must tame the tank and the aeroplane; they've got to be as familiar to us as taxis. Boys must run away to the air as Lord Reading, Masefield and other famous men have run away to sea'. The reviewer commented – he surely had Halton in mind – that the air did hold a wondrous attraction to a youngster whose future had not been determined for him. So why not, he said, a youth whose thoughts have turned to the air leaving his home for say Croydon or whatever airport he has in mind to be the starting point of the great adventure as an airman. Will he, like his predecessor who ran away to sea, become disillusioned or will the sheer romance of it persuade him to adopt the air as his life's career ? Will he, like many who have done the same thing by the sea, rise by ability and close study until his name shall go down to posterity as one of the great air commanders . . . but the vision is so full of glamour that we wish we were many decades younger. We would run away from home to the air![13]

Air Vice-Marshal Sir Ranald Reid (see Foreword) later Air Officer Commanding RAF Halton 1936-1938, was posted to No 1 School of Technical Training in January 1921 – the same month as King George V approved the design of the Royal Air Force Ensign. Reid, the son of a gold prospector, had been credited with the destruction of at least ten enemy aircraft – in 1916 in the course of one week alone, he brought eight down. His unpublished memoirs describe his three years 'at the great RAF engineering Training School at

Halton'. Then aged 28, and a Squadron Leader, he 'helped to administer and control the Chief of the Air Staff Trenchard's revolutionary apprentices' training scheme.' He found it an exhilarating job, working with the splendid types of young men who joined the RAF for this three-year training – educational, technical and disciplinary – with lots of games to keep them fit in lovely country surroundings.[14]

As their squadron commander, Reid in 1921 welcomed the first intake of Halton apprentices to the hutted North Camp. He recalls how gradually four great groups of splendid barracks with ample school and workshop facilities were built at Trenchard's behest to provide a very fine training centre. 'Without this school' he wrote, 'the Royal Air Force could hardly have won their great victories in the second World War. It provided very good ground-staff and many top pilots during the war'.

But conditions for boys at Halton in the early 'twenties was in distinct contrast to that for regular officers. Reid wrote, the senior staff like myself had a good life too [ex-apprentices will raise an eyebrow at the word 'too'] starting with old Dan Scarlett (ex-Royal Navy), the Air Commodore and downwards with Gp Capt Newall (Chief of the Air Staff at the outbreak of World War II) and Ginger Darnell (tough ex-Army Colonel) through a strong staff of officers, civilians, school teachers, technical and administrative officers and nco's. Sir Philip Sassoon, the Air Minister had presented Halton with some polo ponies and the club of which Sdn Ldr Reid was a member included local land-owners and 'copers'. The grass of their polo-ground on the aerodrome was kept well-cropped by a flock of sheep. Hunting was favoured by the 'seniors' and Reid's horse 'Tishy' was purchased from Harry Beauchamp, the famous hunting R.C. parson. Despite so much time in the saddle with the Tring Drag, of which he was Master, or the old Berkely, or the Whaddon Chase, Beauchamp managed to do his job well and, also Reid adds, was a dearly beloved person.

In 1925, Reid commanded RAF Spittlegate whose Group Commander was Bonham-Carter (his influence on Halton is described in Chapter 6). Bonham-Carter, he said, had enormous courage, and always seemed cheerful, *although rather fierce*, [Author's italics] despite the constant pain from a severe wound sustained in the first war when he lost a leg. When Reid was posted back to Halton, this time as AOC, his remark was limited to 'then in '37 to take over the command of dear old Halton and then in September 1938, away overseas again'.[15]

Apart from Halton, by 1924 there were two other centres devoted to the training of aircraft apprentices, one at Cranwell, and the other at Flowerdown (see below), near Winchester. From 1926 there were no boys or apprentices under training at Cranwell until August 1929 with the transfer of the Electrical and Wireless School from Flowerdown whose 15th and last entry had passed out in January that year.

In January 1922 the Amalgamated Engineering Union and Air Ministry officials on the occasion of their visits to the Cranwell workshops and school were most impressed with the facilities and submitted a favorable report. Not long after this visit Lt Col Caldwell, DSO, MA, an education officer, was transferred from Cranwell since it was considered that the experience he had gained there would be invaluable in setting the Halton Boys' School on its feet. Caldwell, a leader in the truest sense of the word, demanded unquestioning loyalty but in return gave an unswerving support to those under him. He retired from the RAF Education Service in 1932 (see Chapter 5). It is of interest that Caldwell was founder of the Old Haltonians Society in 1925.[16]

During 1922 conditions at Halton remained rugged. The wooden huts had no toilet facilities except for night urinal-tubs. Khaki uniforms with army-type boots were still issued as working dress. Much of the first six months training consisted of square-bashing relieved by some basic metalwork at workshops. A short-lived 'Small Boys Squad' was specially trained to march twice as fast as the others in order to keep up with them. One ex-apprentice, who completed his training at Flowerdown, recalls lax NCO's at North Camp being detailed to undergo 'at the double' drill parades with the boys allowed to watch. In December that year, for the passing out at Cranwell of the September 1920 Entry, AVM Swann CB CBE, reviewing officer, spoke of the expansion of the RAF now underway and the opportunities thus open for clever and ambitious young airmen.[17]

Graduation of first Aircraft Apprentices
The first 399 Aircraft Apprentices to complete the three-year apprenticeship, as No 1 Entry, at No 1 School of Technical Training, Halton (under *AO Memo* No 1206) passed out on 17 December 1922 under the eye of their reviewing officer – who else but Air Chief Marshal Sir Hugh Trenchard GCB,DSO, then Chief of Air Staff. The very first Halton Aircraft Apprentice, Sdn Ldr A J Akehurst RAF (Ret'd), whose portrait hangs on the wall of Halton School, was one of eight Fitters Armourer – the original 'plumbers' of the RAF. Trenchard had a personal word for him on parade: 'So you are now an AC1, eh ?' His pride at being spoken to was deflated when the great man added 'Well, I suppose that is **some** sort of start!' [18]

At Cranwell in January 1924 Trenchard, who had been been prevented by family business from attending the passing out parade, sent a message read out by the Commandant. Trenchard reminded those present that the previous year he had not been satisfied with the results – he was still not satisfied and would not be until at least 80% of the apprentices passed out as LAC's. He insisted that the efficiency of the Air Force as a whole depended to a great extent on the efficiency of the products of Cranwell and Halton.

No doubt at the instigation of Messrs Kermode, Needham and Browne, education officers, who had been transferred from Cranwell to Halton, the first Passing-Out Examination at Schools to be held at Halton was in Summer 1924.[19]

At the aerodrome, the Bristol *Fighters* (Bif), DH9A's, Avro *504* trainers, Sopwith *Snipes*, were all outshone by the twin-engined Boulton and Paul *Bugle* which always topped the aerobatic display by looping-the-loop. This amazing aircraft and its successor the *Sidestrand* were the only twin-engine planes to be cleared for full aerobatics up to 1939. Training included hand-starting which on the rotaries, where the whole engine rotated with the propellor, was a precarious business. Most 'dodgy' however, was the DH9A, with its coil ignition, which started with the slightest tug. But the lasting impression of the first ten entries was the stench of burnt castor-oil thrown out by the rotary engines.

The first issue of *The Halton Magazine* (5,000 copies sold) marking the end of Easter term 1924 attracted favorable press comment. The *Aeroplane* of May 21 commented that it was instructive without in the least being dull. The notes on technical training were also of particular interest to outsiders. The same week *Flight* remarked that its journalistic quality was in line with Halton training which they had recently been able to inspect. In the words of the Editor 'it seeks to portray Halton in every mood – Halton the care-worn; Halton the care-free; Halton the grave; Halton the gay; Halton'.

Blue uniforms became universal in 1924, before then working dress was khaki – particularly appreciated for the non-polish buttons. Boots were army 'ammo-type' of stiff brown leather soaked in grease which had somehow to be blacked and polished. Each section (wing) was identified by a strip of tape on each side of the cap-badge which in turn was superseded by brass numerals on the crown of the cap-badge. Fall-in drill on the parade-ground followed a series of drum-beats instead of verbal orders. Each section had its own drum, fife and trumpet band – the pipes did not arrive until 1926. The clockwork stick-drill of the side, tenor and bass drummers with 'stupendous' drum-majors was always impressive.

Fatigues included hated coal-heaving as well as cookhouse duties: hand-peeling of potatoes onions, carrots etc, washing hundreds of dirty plates, in addition to emery-clothing hot-plates and cookers.[20]

Trenchard's pride in his apprentice scheme was again shaken in December 1924, this time at Halton with the passing out of the third entry. *The Times* gave full coverage to his inspection on 17 December including a photograph of Trenchard taking the salute. The great man was far from happy as was evident from the long report 'RAF Training Centre – Developments at Halton'.

The most difficult problem of personnel then facing the Royal Air Force, Trenchard insisted, was ensuring an adequate and steady supply of trained airmen for the maintenance of the highly technical equipment of the Air Service. There was accommodation for 2,000 but that figure was to be doubled so that 4,000 apprentices would be training at Halton at any one time. At the time of Trenchard's inspection, 1,889 'boys' were under training and it was only the lack of barrack accommodation that prevented the transfer of the boys section from Cranwell. Training was carried out on 'comparatively recent types' such as the Fairey *Fawn*, the Parnell *Plover*, and two twin-engined aircraft, one of all-metal construction. The more advanced boys overhauled engines in service use prior to these being inspected and rechecked at a service depot.

Trenchard emphasized that Halton was at last settling down from a period of reorganization and revision of the syllabus to meet the new entry examination system. This explained the poor results achieved by the entry due to pass out that day. Only 136 had graduated from a total of 399. *The Times* emphasized that no attempt had been made to gloss over this which showed that Halton was determined to build up a high standard of efficiency. Halton was endeavouring in three years to accomplish what in industry took five years.

The actual passing out results showed 15 LAC's, 121 AC1's, 191 AC2's and 67 failures. Two cadetships to the RAF College were announced as were the names of 8 'boys' selected to proceed directly for the corporals' course. Trenchard pointed out that very shortly with the exception of the wireless centre at Flowerdown, Halton would be the only centre where aircraft apprentices would be trained. Halton, had developed within the last five years but was nowhere near yet what it would become in the future. He was bitterly disappointed at the examination results from which he had perhaps expected too much. The number of leading aircraftmen and ACI's was far too small. He felt certain that given a further opportunity the AC2's and the failures could pass in a much higher grade. He was authorized to say that they would be given another chance, and would thus be retained at Halton for a further six months. At the end of this time he wanted to see them all, or at least the majority of them pass out as leading aircraftmen. Nothing else was good enough for the Air Service.[21]

The gasps of the 'lucky' 258 apprentices whose three-year stint had thus been extended seem to have been ignored by *The Times* correspondent. Trenchard concluded by saying that some of those passing out, after a year's work, would be selected for training as pilots and would then have a great opportunity opened to them. One apprentice recalls that 14 of those retained at Halton succeeded in passing out as LAC's, much to the annoyance of himself and and many others who were obliged to wait 12 months before they were allowed to sit the examination for reclassification.[22]

On 22 October 1925, No 1 Apprentices Wing, Halton was formed at Hendersen Barracks under Wg Cdr H I Hammer DFC as first Commanding Officer assisted by 7 junior officers, 4 sergeant-majors, 12 sergeants and 18 corporals. The previous title of the unit had been No 1 Boys' Wing, the alteration was authorized under *AMWO* 649/25 and promulgated in Halton Command Orders Serial Number 239 (27.10.1925). By this same order No 2 Section was renamed No 2 Apprentices Wing. As it was the first unit at Halton to train apprentices, it should in fact have been designated No 1 Wing. The first nominated commanding officer of No 2 Wing from 1927 to 1930 was Wg Cdr D Harries AFC.[23]

After attestation and kitting out, apprentices in the wireless and instruments groups were posted to Flowerdown and Cranwell for technical training. The remaining apprentices were then distributed between Nos 1 and 2 Wings Halton. However, as this did not prove practicable it was decided that a complete entry would be allocated to one or other of the two Wings, in this way each Wing henceforth had a Junior and Senior Entry. Later, within each Wing apprentices were assigned to three squadrons, A,B or C, depending upon whether they were rated above average, average, or below average.[24]

Boys' Wing Cranwell

In August 1925 T E Lawrence, who had enlisted as an airman in the Royal Air Force, was posted to B Flight at the Cadet College Cranwell. In his book *The Mint*, he describes the AOC Air Cdre 'Biffy' Borton CB CMG DSO AFC with whom he had served in the desert and who had governed cities and planned battles. His nonchalant 'Cawwy on, Sergeant Major' before strolling off the parade ground delighted the ranks of airmen and apprentices.

Air Cdre Borton was Commandant of RAF Cranwell during the period August 1921 to 1926. Following Cambridge, he had transferred from his Highland Regiment to No 5 Squadron RFC in 1914. His immediate predecessor, Air Commodore CAH Longcraft MG DSO AFC (1921/2) – who thought only of hunting, flying and Cranwell – in 1920 had launched the first number of the *RAF College Magazine*. Meanwhile, the *Boys' Wing Magazine* continued to report on activities at Cranwell up to 1926, at which date the 'mechanical' apprentices moved to Halton. During that year, the newly promoted Air Vice Marshal FC Halahan CMG CBE DSO MVO took over as the new Commandant of RAF Cranwell, where he remained until 1929.

In September 1923, Air Commodore Sir Frank Whittle commenced training at Cranwell as an apprentice rigger. A fuller outline of his RAF apprentice training, and incidentally his meeting with T E Lawrence at Cranwell, is given in Appendix G. It was an historic occasion when the world's first successful jet aircraft took off from Cranwell aerodrome in 1941. At the age of 22 Whittle had applied for his patent for a turbo-jet engine, but he very nearly missed having an Air Force career when he failed his medical examination as an aircraft apprentice at Halton in 1922.

Whittle who had passed the written Aircraft Apprentices' examination had been three inches short of the minimum height requirement of five feet. After succesfully following for several months a course of physical training exercises at the hands of an ex-army instructor, he again applied for admission but was informed that he could not be permitted a second chance. He decided that to reapply would be the simplest way of gaining admission and following this second attempt he was accepted.

The training undertaken as an Aircraft Apprentice undoubtedly formed a valuable basis for Whittle's subsequent education during his two years' as a

Flight Cadet. As he put it, 'as in the Apprentices' Wing, school subjects were broadly divided into two groups', the one covering English literature and history; and the other including physics, mathematics and theory of flight. On the practical side, workshop training dealt with repair and maintenance but although more broadly based was not so thorough. It is not surprizing that all ex-apprentices selected for Cranwell cadetships passed out with flying colours particularly, as remarked by Air Cdre Borton, cadets had little or no scientific knowledge [25]

Cranwell continued to train the overflow of fitters and riggers, as they were then called, from 1923 until 1926, by which date the barracks, workshops and school which made up the training centre at Halton had been completed. The Cranwell apprentices who transferred to Halton to continue their airframe or engine training moved into No 4 Wing in August 1926. The Halton apprentices who looked forward to meeting them included Jerry Partridge (13th Entry). He recalls that the 4th to 7th Entries housed in Nos 1 and 2 Wings had just returned from summer leave. Both wings had formed up on the parade ground for the Colour Hoisting Parade, each accompanied by their trumpet and fife bands. The parade waited patiently for the duty officer to take up his position with the two trumpeters in front of the flagstaff to take the salute. Suddenly from the direction of No 4 Wing they heard a double-three drum-roll (instead of the usual five-roll beat) followed by a wail which drew a smile from all the Scotsmen on parade – **the pipes had come to Halton**! [26]

The 600 members of Whittle's entry, No 8 Cranwell, was the last to complete its three-year training period at Cranwell. The move of the six remaining entries of 'apprentice mechanicals' from Cranwell (No's 9 to 14) undoubtedly represented a heavy logistic burden for the administrative headquarters at both units as well as complicating the entry numbering system at Halton. By way of example, the Reverend Stanley Coulson, now over eighty, who retired as a squadron leader before entering the church and who had started at Halton with the 6th Entry in September 1925, in a personal letter wrote that members of his entry were proud to call themselves the 6th/12th.[27]

Surprisingly, that autumn the RAF Cadet College in their Magazine under 'College Notes' gave pride of place to the departure of the Apprentices' Wing from Cranwell:

> '. . . It is impossible to say here how much we shall miss this magnificent unit. It is typical of it, and particularly of its relations with us, that the boy apprentices as a parting gift should bave presented to the Flight-Cadets a magnificent trophy, for their Mess, to be offered annually as a trophy for inter-squadron rowing. We wish the Wing as great a success at Halton as they had at Cranwell. We are sorry that they are going.' [28]

The twelth and last issue of the Cranwell *Boys' Wing Magazine*, under its once-only title *No 4 Apprentices Wing Magazine*, [the Boys' Wing had become

No 4 (Apprentices) Wing in October 1925, and in August 1926 continued to be known as such on transfer to Halton which, curiously, lacked a No 3 Wing until its formation in 1930] contained a foreword from Air Cdre Borton. After expressing regret that this was the final number of the journal, he said he was confident that following its move to Halton, the Wing would maintain the same traditions and earn the same opinion that it had so amply justified in the past. In the same issue, the last in a series of what had become known as 'The Halton Letter' appeared:

> '*To the Editor, No 4 Apprentices Wing Magazine*
> This is Halton's last letter to Cranwell, and it is difficult to know quite what to say. All thoughts and ideas are submerged by the fact that after leave the *Cranwell Magazine* will be no more than a glorious memory, and that Cranwell will have moved to Halton. It is inevitable that for you this must have its sad features. We are most happily circumstanced, since your loss of entity is our gain. It has always been a practical ideal to regard Cranwell and Halton as one. The geographical unity now pending gives us every encouragement in hoping that this ideal is capable of great achievement, and in extending to all, old friends and new, the heartiest of welcomes we look to the future with hope and with confidence. Cranwell has proved its vigour and its worth in six years of steady growth and expansion. It has made its influence felt all over the Empire, where the Air Force flies. Its work and its spirit can never die.
>
> For our part, we have very little to report since your last issue. The new building and barracks to 'house' you are now practically complete, and we are confident you will like them. We have also had the pleasure of welcoming Cranwell representatives to various conferences during the past few months, and as we write your colleague, Mr Hutchinson, [Lt Cdr, who had moved to Halton in June 1926] is busy superintending the off-loading of your first consignment of stores and furniture. Finally, as it seems quite impossible for me to get away from the one and only topic of the Great Move, I would like to quote the lines of welcome written by Mr E C Classon in the forthcoming issue of our *Halton Magazine*:
>
> > Cranwell, you come to us in all your glory,
> > Older than we, but wiser for your age,
> > Here to resume the making of your story,
> > With Halton by you on the title page.
> > Your needs are ours, and ours in yours are blended:

Both to the Service must subservient lie,
And self-forgetting seize the chance extended,
Each moulding each in mutual destiny.
All vain regrets upon the common altar
Of Service welfare must together stand,
And our unswerving purpose never falter –
To build a greater Halton, hand in hand.'

Halton debated in The House of Commons

Discussion of the *Air Estimates* early in 1926 included a number of detailed interventions from back-benchers. Several members had visited RAF Halton following an invitation by the AOC Air Vice-Marshal Lambe. Sir Frank Nelson referred to the 1,781 apprentices then under training which on completion of the building that September would shortly rise to the establishment of 3,000. The total administrative personnel of 940 included 66 officers, 737 airmen, 106 civilians and 31 educational staff. He added the remark that 'with the greatest respect and deference' a number of colleagues in the House had felt that the latter total compared with the roster of 1,781 apprentices – a ratio of two to one – called for some explanation. In particular he failed to understand why 737 airmen at Halton were necessary to carry out the fatigue duties in the dormitories, kitchens, etc, when by extending their training time by a month or so this work could be undertaken by the apprentices.

On the other hand, while he agreed that the finest technical education in the world was now given in the three years' course at Halton he wondered whether the cost could be reduced. In this way, although it might have been excellent for recruiting, perhaps the Under-Secretary could explain why at the Halton Parents' Day the previous year 7,000 parents had received tea. Furthermore he failed to understand why a large aerodrome with 15 aircraft was found necessary for training ground staff even though they could have 'what is technically known as a flip once a year'. The staff could very well do their several hours of regular flying at neighbouring aerodromes.

Furthermore, he had calculated that the cost to the country of training one apprentice at Halton was £230 per annum. This figure was greater than it cost a parent to send a boy to leading public schools in England where the ratio of administrative staff to pupils was five to one. The cost for his own son at Winchester averaged only £65 a term. In addition, the apprentices received one shilling a day pocket money most of which was spent in the canteen and which, when they numbered 3,000, would cost a further £55,000 a year. Half that amount for lads of 15 to 18 years of age, in his view, should be adequate and better for their digestions. He reminded the Under-Secretary of State for Air that on Friday, which was pay day, 'the evening meal at Halton Park is completely knocked off because there is so much pay received that no meal is needed at all'.

Sir Philip Sassoon, in reply, said they were halfway through a large expansion programme with 25 squadrons operational out of an authorised total of 52. The first problem was to build the sheds, hangars and aerodromes from which to fly the aircraft. Before spending between three and fifteen thousand pounds each on aeroplanes, the mechanics and engineers had to be trained and schools and workshops provided. In other words, the foundations had to be laid before putting on the tiles. He had seen photographs in the newspapers showing Air Force cadets marching past in review and lampooned as 'The Royal Ground Force'. But he wondered whether it was appreciated that at Halton only two and a half hours a week were devoted to drill. Whereas at the end of the war 84 men had been required to keep one machine in the air, the figure had now been reduced to 50. As regards accommodation, 80% of the total personnel in the RAF were still housed in temporary buildings. In reply to the criticisms about fatigues, if the apprentices themselves did these then they would spend less time on training. Also, a reduction in their pay would mean that the Government would have to provide railway warrants when they went on leave. The aerodrome at Halton was essential since apprentices had to learn how to swing propellors and handle aeroplanes as they would have to do on the squadrons.

Brig-Gen Charteris stated that all the services considered a Ministry of Defence would sooner or later be necessary. After objecting to Admiral Sueter's comment about the Army making people wear spurs, he called for explanations on why Halton cost more to administer than the whole of the Aldershot Command. Mr Charleton, another private member, referred to his recent visit to Halton and as a mechanical engineer he had been delighted with what he had seen. There was no such thing as a square peg in a round hole, and if a lad could not progress in one trade he was transferred to another. One visitor had commented, 'If this was being done in my railway, we should do it by machinery'. The RAF officer had replied 'Yes, but your machinery would not be in the Sahara Desert or on the plains of Iraq, and we are training these men to do the work without machinery.' Another Army officer, Brig Gen Warner, also in the party that had recently visited Halton, considered that the apprentices were very fortunate to be undergoing the training. He said 'I was so struck with every one of the boys that I saw, that I recognised that they would form a fine basis of pilots for the Royal Air Force, and I would suggest to the Minister that every one of these boys who go through this apprenticeship, apart from those who go as Cadets to Cranwell, should be given this advantage'.

In a long speech towards the end of the debate on the *Air Estimates*, Sir Samuel Hoare, Secretary of State for Air, disagreed with the idea that an engineering branch should be set up in the Air Force. He preferred the ideal, even though it might be difficult to attain, of spreading engineering knowledge through the whole service and trying to make all airmen to some extent engineers ... Engineeering standards in the Air Force were getting higher every year.

At the close of the discussions it was resolved that the Air Force should be maintained with 35,000 all ranks, exclusive of those serving in India, for the service during the year ending 31 March 1927.[29]

On 16 December 1926, Wing Commander C D Breese, AFC, who as an Engineer Lieutenant had been one of the first naval officers to join the RNAS, read an important paper 'The training of Aircraft Apprentices' to the Royal Aeronautical Society in London. This paper summarized in Appendix D gives an excellent picture of the academic side of Halton at this period. Wg Cdr Breese, who had been responsible for the technical examination of potential officers for the RNAS or RFC, was in charge of the technical training of all apprentices. Before the paper was given, the Chairman announced that the Council of the Royal Aeronautical Society had decided that an annual prize to be known as the Elliott Memorial Prize would be given for competition among the apprentices under training at Halton.[30]

The Flowerdown Apprentices

A history of the Halton system would not be complete without mention of the Flowerdown Apprentices with their plum-coloured distinguishing hat bands. For the full story of this pioneer school the reader is referred to the Bibliography. As the first RAF Electrical and Wireless School had began training apprentices from January 1922, its traditions were maintained at the Electrical and Wireless School Cranwell from 1927 to 1952 and then at No 1 Radio School Locking until 1970. In the 1920's, conditions at Halton and Cranwell were undoubtedly demanding but not comparable with those at Flowerdown. One ex-apprentice of the 9th Entry, Gp Capt WTH Nichols, spent most of the war as a prisoner in a Japanese POW Camp. He attributed his survival to his Flowerdown training, 'after three years of that' he said, 'the Nips could not shake me!'

To give only one example of Flowerdown's efficiency, in December 1925, Sir Philip Sassoon inspected the RAF Wireless and Electrical School. A photograph in *The Times* shows the apprentices parading on the grass sports field as they marched past. Results were better than those obtained at Halton and of those passing out there was not a single failure. Three entries had now been sent to the Central Trade Testing Board and in no case had there been a failure. Of the 290 apprentices under training 40 were now passing out of which 9 were LAC's, 20 ACI's and 11 ACII's. Four had been retained to undergo a further advanced course before being promoted corporals. Sir Philip was delighted that every one of those who had passed out had volunteered to become airmen pilots.

After attestation at Halton, entrants of above average ability particularly in mathematics and science were selected from apprentices for the technical skills required to master the new technology of wireless and electrical engineering. Of the 745 apprentices to pass through Flowerdown no less than 65% were commissioned. A total of one hundred made wing commander or higher, including nine who reached air rank. A large proportion of the Flowerdown apprentices became aircrew and it is known that 157 were killed on air operations during the war.[32]

NOTES

4 Early days Halton/Cranwell (1919-1926)

1   Air 2/129 XC 22757; AHB (66) Memo 1338; Haslam, op cit, pp 19-22

2   *Flight*, 20.11.1919; NOTE An Appendix to Air 2/129 XC 22757 announced an open competitive examination (Maths, science English and general knowledge) for the entry of Boy Mechanics, '. . . identical with that held for the entry of boy artificers and apprentices for service under the Admiralty'. The conditions of service for 1921 entrants stipulated: 'Boy Mechanics are attested for twelve years' service *from date of entry* [Author's italics], consisting of ten years regular Air Force service, and two years in the reserve'. Compared with subsequent conditions of service, pay was generous: Boy Mechanics were to be paid 1s 6d per day until the age of 18, when the rate rose to 3 shillings a day. On completing the course of training they would receive immediate promotion to Leading Aircraftman and be paid 5s 6d per day. Those selected for the advanced course for immediate promotion to corporal would get 7s 9d a day.

3   *The Haltonian*, Summer 1984 (L H Weeks, Boy Mechanic)

4   *Command Document* 467 (Dec 1919) quoted by Armitage, op cit. *The Times* 17.12.1919

5   Air 8/10 10.6.1919

6   *ibid*, 11.11.1919

7   AMWO 9/1920 (AHB)

8   RAF Museum, MS Egles

9   *The Haltonian*, Summer 1984 (L H Weeks Boy Mechanic). *ibid*, Summer 1990 (Phil Kingston)

10   Air 2/140/152166/20, Armitage, op cit, Air 2/Box 142 180071/20

11   Haslam, op cit, p 43; Armitage, op cit

12   *The Times*, 2.8.1920

13   *Flight*, 20.10.1921

14   AHB

15   AVM Sir Ranald Reid, Unpublished memoirs, Imperial War Museum, 88/30/1

16   *Boys' Wing Magazine*, Spring 1922, *The Halton Magazine* Summer 1932; Kimber, op cit, p 95; Haslam, op cit p 45.
      NOTE: The name Old Cranwellians first used by the Boys' Wing Association Cranwell in 1923 predates by three years the Association of

that name formed by the Cadet College. Thus the term 'Old Cranwellian' could refer equally to an ex-Apprentice or an ex-Cadet.

17 Burch, op cit, pp 127/128; *Boys' Wing Magazine*, Xmas 1923
18 *The Halton Magazine*, Spring 1968 (Sdn Ldr A. J. Akhurst).
19 *Boys' Wing Magazine*, Easter 1924
20 *The Halton Magazine*, Winter 1959; *ibid*, Spring 1960 (Sdn Ldr E E Swinbourne 3rd Entry)
    NOTE: From the first entry of apprentices in 1922, Nos 1, 2 and 4 Wings had been identified by a brass numeral above the cap-badge, while a coloured cap-band denoted the squadron. But as from 6 December 1928, cap-bands indicated the wing: green (for No 1 Wing), light blue (for No 2 Wing) and red (for No 4 Wing). A black, white or yellow disc behind the cap-badge designated A, B or C squadron. With the expansion in 1936 and the creation of No 3 Wing and re-establishment (after five years) of No 4 Wing, hat-band colours became: No 1 Wing – green; No 2 Wing – red; No 3 Wing – chequered red and navy-blue; No 4 Wing – yellow; No 5 Wing – chequered red and green. Coloured discs behind cap-badges still designated squadrons (A, B or C). By this time, other Apprentice Schools had been set up including Ruislip for Apprentice Clerks which had adopted the previous light-blue (after repeated scrubbing they became white) hat-bands of No 2 Wing and red for the Apprentice School at Cranwell.
21 Also in *The Aeroplane*, 24.12.1924
22 Air 29/738; *The Haltonian*, Winter 1991 (Sydney Harris)
23 Kimber, op cit, p 84
24 Air 29/728; Kimber, op cit, pp 82,83
25 Whittle, op cit, pp 11/12 ; Haslam, op cit, p 35
26 *The Haltonian*, Winter 1990 (Jerry Partridge)
27 NOTE: The full listing covering Entries Nos 1 to 14 showing original locations and service numbers prepared by Alan Small, Secretary of the RAF Halton Aircraft Apprentices Association, is given in *The Haltonian*, Winter 1990.
28 *Royal Air Force Cadet College Magazine*, Autumn 1926
29 *Hansard*, Vol 192, Feb/Mar 1926, pp 820-876
    NOTE
    Sir Samuel Hoare in the Air Estimates debate of the previous year (*Hansard*, Vol 181, March 1925, pp 1671/3) had already rejected the concept of an engineering branch for the RAF. He had considered that the education of Halton apprentices was as good as any education given to boys of a similar age at any school in the country. As a former member of the Education Committee of the London County Council, during an earlier visit to Halton, instead of finding gaps in their education he had been amazed at the excellence of their training, and advised those in doubt to visit Halton and to judge for themselves whether his testimony was justified.

30 NOTE
    Elliott Memorial Prize. The Chairman of the Royal Aeronautical Society
    explained that the late Mr Arthur Elliott, a former mechanic in the RAF,
    after joining the De Havilland Company had flown with Sir Alan Cobham
    on his earlier long distance flights. The success of Sir Alan Cobham,
    particularly his flight to Tangier and the King's Cup Race of 1924, had
    been in no small measure due to the wonderful work of Mr Elliott.
    Returning from one long flight when he had been wounded in the air, the
    barely conscious Elliott, had warned Cobham to see that the oil supply to
    the engine was turned off.
31 *The Times*, 19.12.1925
32 Kimber, op cit, pp 105-108; Sdn Ldr L L R Burch, *The Flowerdown Link*,
    op cit, pp 45/46; Frank Whitehouse, *The Poacher's Brats,* op cit.

il

Chapter Five

THE PEACEFUL YEARS (1927-1936)

On 11 January 1927, Trenchard inspected the 576 apprentices of the '4th Entry to complete the course at Halton', renumbered (as explained above) the 10th to include the Cranwell entries. Forty apprentices who had originally enlisted at Halton had been posted to Flowerdown for training as wireless operator mechanics. Although 43 apprentices were classified as Leading Aircraftsmen 72 had failed the course. Besides the award of three cadetships, twelve boys were selected for the advanced course for promotion to corporal. This accelerated promotion for 'ready-made NCO's', a step which in the 'twenties could take up to five years, was not well-received in the RAF and had to be discontinued.

The report approved of the disciplinary standard of the 1924 Entry but hoped that once the 'System Unit Training by Wings' was in force there would be 'further improvement in routine marching in the Halton Camp'. The 95 carpenter-riggers had completely constructed three *Grebe* aircraft using metal fittings taken from crashed aircraft.

Following the parade, Trenchard congratulated the 3,000 boys in the large gymnasium on their fine discipline and bearing. He told them 'he hoped one day that a boy apprentice trained at Halton would occupy his chair [Author's Note: on 15 October 1982 an ex-Cranwell apprentice, Air Chief Marshal Sir Keith Williamson – who retired from the active list as Marshal of the Royal Air Force – was appointed Chief of the Air Staff, joining Sir John Rogers, another ex-Cranwell apprentice, who retired as Air Chief Marshal] The Air Service, he said, was extensive and each member could not be mothered, so that each had to help themselves. Now that a boys' wing had been transferred from Cranwell, Halton was the final conception of what a training station should be.[1]

At the beginning of 1927, according to recruiting announcements 3,500 apprentices had already entered the Royal Air Force, which figure one year later had reached 5,000.[2]

At this juncture, a new grouping within Wings was introduced so that an entire entry was attached to one specific Wing. In this way, No 1 Wing housed the January 1925 entry (Halton) and the September, 1926, entry referred to as the 11th and 14th entries respectively. No 2 Wing housed the September, 1925 (Halton) entry, and the January 1927, known as the 11th and 15th entries. No 4 Wing included the September 1924 entry (Cranwell) and the January 1926 entry (Halton) referred to as the 10th and 13th entries.[3]

Trenchard was again on parade in 1927 for the passing out of the 6th/12th: Jan 1925 Entry. The full coverage of the ceremony in *The Aeroplane* of 28 December reported that a thick layer of frozen snow on the parade ground had prevented the usual passing out ceremony and marchpast from being held. Nevertheless, 2434 apprentices from the three wings heard the commandant AVM C L Lambe refer to the complete redrafting of the advanced training syllabus and the reorganization of entries that had taken place in January that year. Discipline and drill had not reached the requisite standard since their NCO's were 10% below the barely adequate establishment.

During the tour of the workshops, Trenchard had been shown the *Mayfly* biplane – a Certificate of Airworthiness had been issued in June – entirely designed and constructed at Halton. The *Mayfly*, converted to a successful monoplane the following year, is described in Appendix E.

In his address, commenting on this sixth entry to pass into the Royal Air Force, he said they would bring the total of ex-apprentices, trained at either Cranwell or Halton, up to 4,000, and he hoped that they were beginning to make their weight felt in the Service. On the question of ceremonial functions and drill he emphasized that he did not want a lot of drill. On the other hand, what he did want was the best that could be obtained from intelligence. In this connection, he did not quite understand why there should be any difference between technical and educational training since it all came under the heading of education. He quoted figures showing how the standard had improved but insisted there should be at least 25% LAC's and virtually no failures at graduation. He presented a prize and a Wakefield Scholarship to No 365737 Aircraft Apprentice A E Earle – who was to become Air Chief Marshal Sir Alfred Earle, and Vice-Chief of the Defence Staff – one of four apprentices offered cadetships to the RAF College Cranwell and whom he addressed privately after the ceremony.[4]

In May 1927 the Chief Scout, Sir Robert Baden-Powell, on the occasion of a visit, said that Halton was not a barrack-square in some smoky city but stood high in the beechwoods on the hills overlooking the Vale of Aylesbury. It was a wonderful place and of the 2,500 apprentices under training added 'and very smart they look, too'. They were paid one shilling a day, he said, rising to one shilling and sixpence, and after Halton as a sergeant it could rise to nine shillings and sixpence. In response to his request to meet apprentices who had once been Boy Scouts, he was astonished to see more than 400 who paraded for his benefit. 'A jolly fine lot they looked' he commented, 'well set up, disciplined, smart as paint, and underneath as jolly as sandboys – whatever sandboys may be !'[5] Later that year, another distinguished visitor was HRH

Princess Mary who opened the new RAF Hospital with 204 beds, complete with operating theatre and x-ray department.[6]

The annual *Air Estimates* invariably refer to apprentice training, and show how increasing reliance was placed on that system of forming ground engineers. In this way, provision was made in 1926 for 208 airmen pilots, many of whom were ex-apprentices. The *Estimates* also called for 96 boys to begin training as apprentice clerks (there had been an experimental entry of Boy Clerks in 1921) at Ruislip, the home of the RAF Record Office. The apprentice clerks which had come into existence in 1925, again thanks to Lord Trenchard's foresight, continued until the last entry No 61 passed out in 1942. By that date a total of 2,080 apprentice clerks had been trained of which a high proportion were either commissioned or became aircrew. After the war came the administrative apprentices' scheme but this is outside the scope of this book.[7]

By 1927 the established number of airmen pilots had increased to 242, who in addition to their flying duties would be eligible to carry out certain technical duties which had previously been performed by officers. After five years' flying service they were to return to their normal ground trades but remain in flying practice and be liable for flying duties in war. The reserve of short-service officers was correspondingly reduced by this substitution of airmen pilots for officers. It was reported that the boys training establishment at Cranwell had been transferred to Halton, where all aircraft apprentices would be trained in future except those instructed in electrical and wireless trades, who would remain at the Electrical and Wireless School at Flowerdown. This concentration of aircraft apprentice training at Halton, which had resulted in definite administrative savings, was the final realisation of the policy first laid down in 1919.

The 1928 *Air Estimates* announced that the Electrical and Wireless School, where officers and airmen were trained in signals duties and where aircraft apprentices entered for training in the electrical and wireless trades on a three-year course, was moving from Flowerdown to Cranwell. The Cranwell command now included the Royal Air Force College (previously designated the Royal Air Force Cadet College) and the Electrical and Wireless School.

At RAF Cranwell between the years 1926 to 1929 there were no apprentices under training. Meanwhile, the apprentices whose training had continued from 1922 onwards at the Electrical and Wireless School, Flowerdown, on its closure in 1929 moved to No 2 Electrical and Wireless School, Cranwell, which had reopened for apprentice training. The history of the Cranwell apprentices up to their move to No 1 Radio School, Locking, in 1950 until its final closure in 1974, has been adequately dealt with by Frank Whitehouse in his two books dealing with the history of the Apprentices at Cranwell.

According to the 1929 *Estimates*, Aircraft apprentices and apprentice clerks who entered at about the age of 16 for training to fill the technical and clerical trades respectively would continue to be recruited for 12 years' active list service, counting from the age of 18, with no reserve liability.

Air Commodore I M Bonham-Carter CB, OBE (1928-1931)

The legendary Bonham-Carter after service in South Africa and India as an infantry officer had lost a leg in France. He had flown with No 5 Squadron RFC in an aircraft modified so that the rudder was controlled by a wheel mounted on the control column. With the rank of Lieutenant Colonel he became the first commandant of the RFC units at Halton (as mentioned above) including the School of Technical Training (Men), Airwomen trainees, and the Boys' Training Camp.

Then as Group Captain commanding the RAF Depot, Uxbridge in 1922 he seems to have incurred the dislike of T E Lawrence (352087 A/C Ross) then undergoing initial square-bashing. He unkindly described Bonham-Carter as 'only the shards of a man – left leg gone, a damaged eye and brain (as we charitably suppose), one crippled arm, silver plate and corsets about his ribs...' In the chapter 'Our commanding officer' of *The Mint*, Lawrence recounts his sufferings as headquarters' runner to Bonham-Carter who in all fairness probably resented having 'Lawrence of Arabia'- albeit with Trenchard's permission – dumped among the recruits.

With Lawrence following the Commandant 'like Mary's lamb, two paces behind him', the day began with inspection of a kit layout. While Lawrence did his best to keep in step 'with his dotting false leg', he watched the Commandant while he scattered the kits from three successive beds with his walking stick. At the end of the day Lawrence was driven back to the Commandant's house clinging 'ape-like between the hood and the luggage rack'. As Lawrence walked back to the Camp he could hear him 'loudly drilling his little children in the garden'. One day when Bonham-Carter's three leashed dogs pulled him to the ground nobody went to his aid. Lawrence most disrespectfully repeated the muttering of the watching airmen on the parade ground.

Promoted Air Commodore, Bonham-Carter returned to Halton as AOC from 1928 to 1931. Although Lawrence's opinion was undoubtedly harsh there is no doubt that he was a most unusual commander. A number of apprentices have recounted their personal experiences while acting as his personal runner for the day. One ex-apprentice of the 24th Entry, H Rawlinson, remembered him from sports afternoons on the playing fields mounted on his white horse when 'woe betide you if he was not saluted, even though he often wore civilian clothes . . .' [8]

Another apprentice (en route for the Electrical and Wireless School, Cranwell) remembers on arrival at Wendover Station in August 1931 being 'welcomed' by Bonham-Carter. Clutching their suitcases, after straggling out into the station yard, the new boys were shepherded towards the lorries waiting to take them up to the camp. Meanwhile 'in the middle of the yard, completely alone, stood a one-legged senior officer who did not appear to be enjoying the spectacle one little bit'.[9]

Wg Cdr Kimber recalls an occasion on the King's Birthday Parade when despite his wooden leg, the AOC mounted on a polo pony, cantered over to a section of the parade to express his displeasure. During his second year at Halton, Kimber who had just made his first flight, omitted to salute the Air Commodore who was driving past the aerodrome. After saying how much he had enjoyed the flight, Bonham-Carter smilingly commented 'Good, but you are on the ground now.'

Later that year, Kimber found himself appointed AOC's orderly for the day and accompanied Bonham-Carter who now walked with the help of two sticks. He had been warned by the Personal Assistant not to show any over-solicitude. Bonham-Carter had heard that Kimber's father had survived three sinkings in the Navy in one hour, first on the *Aboukir*, the *Hogue*, and then the *Creasy*. During his tour of inspection of the workshops, Bonham-Carter recounted to several officers that Kimber was the son of a survivor who had been torpedoed three times in one hour. At the end of the day the Air Commodore surprisingly called Kimber into his office and thanked him.[10]

The late Air Commodore I M Bonham-Carter, CB, OBE.
(Kimber, Son of Halton, 1977, pp 42-43 – via HAA.)

In 1930, A L Holland (also in the 17th Entry) had a similar experience. From time to time, on the lines of the Royal Marines' or Guards' ceremony of beating the retreat, the wing band had paraded in 'best blue' for the 'Reveille' parade. Lord Thomson, the Secretary of State was due to inspect the camp that day and as the 'duty boy' had been rejected as too scruffy, Holland already spick and span was dispatched at the double to headquarters, where under the Commandant's eagle eye he was again inspected. He was astonished when the great man said, not unkindly, 'Off with your jacket, lad', and to his Personal Assistant 'fetch the cleaning box.' In Holland's words 'I don't suppose there are many who can boast of having their brasses cleaned by an Air Commodore . . . he also helped with the patent leather shoulder-pouch which was my badge of office for the day.' [11]

Another 16-year old apprentice, Walter Pearce, on his last half-mile of a cross-country run, literally ran up against Bonham-Carter. With the the Officers' Mess just in sight he was climbing slowly over the iron fence when up galloped Bonham-Carter on his white horse. The Commandant listened while Pearce gave his reasons for not jumping the fence – first because it was too high and also the fact that he was too tired. Dismounting from his horse, Bonham-Carter handed him the reins and then counting the paces retreated from the fence. With one hand supporting his good leg he managed to clear the fence before ordering the apprentice to do the same, but twice. Long afterwards, as a patient in the officers' ward of Princess Mary's RAF Hospital, Pearce noticed on a table in the ward a silver ashtray. On it was inscribed a message from Bonham-Carter expressing his thanks to all those in the hospital who had looked after him.[12]

A member of the newly arrived 19th Entry in January 1929, recalls Bonham-Carter standing stiff as a ramrod on the snow-covered parade ground of No 4 Wing while delivering his formal address of welcome to the boys – some of whom in shorts had blue knees from the cold. In 1930, Bonham-Carter's son was tragically killed while blowing up tree stumps. This together with his war injuries resulted in Bonham-Carter's retirement from the Royal Air Force on 1 October 1931, on which day Air-Vice Marshal N D MacEwen CMG DSO assumed command of Halton.[13]

Recalled in March 1940, Bonham-Carter served with distinction during the Battle of Britain before finally retiring the next year. He was buried with full military honours at the Church of St.Michael and All Angels, Halton on 5 January 1954. The Obituary notice in the *The Halton Magazine* remarked that even twenty-five years after his arrival at Halton as Commandant there was always someone who would say 'old Bonham wouldn't have stood for that !'

Reorganization for economic reasons

In 1932 details were given of the reorganization for economic reasons of the School of Technical Training at Halton. This was 'on a basis of two wings (instead of three as at present) in the light of the reduced intake of Aircraft Apprentices, and substantial economy in instructional staff is thus rendered possible.' The *Air Estimates* emphasised, however, that there would be no lowering of the high standard of training given.

During the following year, the *Estimates* refer to 'a large reduction in the number of apprentices entered yearly for training at Halton. Those not re-engaging at the end of their twelve years' service could elect to serve four years on the Reserve with a gratuity of £100. Apprentices would now receive instruction on both airframes and engines, with provision for ex-apprentices to return to Halton for a year's advanced course to qualify them for more responsible duties. This dual training continued in fact until 1938 when following the introduction of more sophisticated aircraft and the need for accelerated training it became necessary to revert to the separate specialisations on airframes and engines.

The following poem, signed C.L.M. (who had presumably failed the scanning course) gives a good picture of the impact of an ex-Halton apprentice on the 'real air force' of the 1930's. It first appeared in *The Daedulus*, magazine of the Old Boys' Association RAF Halton formed in 1925 by Lt Col A F S Caldwell DSO, MA, Principal of the Halton School from 1926 to 1932. The piece was reproduced at the time in the *Cadet College Magazine*, Cranwell, under the heading 'Another Rhyme of the RAF':

THE 'OLD BOY'
The ex-apprentice quits the school
Where life, he thought, was 'ard and crool',
And, filled with vitamins and 'pep',
Enters the world with jaunty step,
To taste that glory justly due,
To L.A.C (or A.C.2).
No less a transformation this is,
Than when small grubs from chrysalises
Emerge to gratify our eyes,
No longer grubs, but butterflies.
(Forgive my muse, that rudely dubs
Our young apprentices mere grubs;
But they themselves, a few years hence,
Will find the term gives no offence!)
New fledged with liberty and cash,
The ex-apprentice cuts a dash,
And grows, perhaps a small moustache;
Thus when he swaggers down the street,
Old ladies murmur, 'Look, how sweet!'

And everybody stands and stares,
Exclaiming 'Is it Owen Nares?'
Pursuing still his bold career,
He dares to drink a glass of beer,
And boast that very soon, by cripe,
He means to learn to smoke a pipe,
And play a game of half-penny nap.
Was ever such a reckless chap?
The ex-apprentice runs his Flight;
He puts the Sergeant-Major right;
With self-assurance hard to match
He keeps the Air Force up to scratch,
Well knowing that if *he* did not,
The bally show would run to pot.
And now, wherever he may go,
Good luck to him, and cheerio.

In addition to Trenchard's presence at the passing out parade of No 11 Entry on 20 December 1928, the other event of the year was the Halton Pageant. The flying display included several light aircraft races, aerobatics and an air combat between opposing *Siskins*. Light relief was provided by 'aerial tennis', described by *Flight* as less amusing than expected. The final item was the bombing by Bristol *Fighters* of a 'hostile native tribe', with an aside by Flight 'What should we do without 'hostile native tribes ?' The parade of massed drums (forty can be counted in the photograph) must have been an impressive sight. A physical training display by apprentices, with no words of command, the timing being set by the Band of the Royal Air Force, Halton Command, was described as excellent.[14]

Also that year, under Mr A C Kermode (see Appendix D) the Halton Debating Society produced a highly successful musical comedy, with dance band and orchestra, 'Time Flies' written and stage managed by members of the educational staff. The 'time machine', reviewed in *Flight*, takes three apprentices both backwards and forwards in time. Despite the attractions of wireless telephony and television the heroes finally opt for Halton life in 1928 A.D.[15]

In 1930, the Debating Society had another hit with their comic opera 'Flat Out' again written and produced by Kermode. An announcement in *Flight* remarked upon the life and vigour with which the show was produced with its astonishingly good orchestra of 25 apprentices. The songs which it said ought to be perpetuated included 'In a Military Way', 'Homesickness', 'Trial Flight' and 'March of the Airmen'.[16]

On 17 December 1931 it was reported in *The Times* that Air Marshal Sir Geoffrey Salmond attended the passing out parade of the 19th Entry.

Although 50 apprentices had passed out as LAC's, 269 as ACI's and 61 as ACII's, and only two had failed with 11 on the sick list, the Commanding Officer said that their standard of training was not quite up to that of their predecessors.

During the 'depression' years with the services contracting, between January 1931 and August 1934 the strength of the 23rd to 30th entries arriving at Halton totalled only 2,320 apprentices – an average of about 300 apprentices per entry. From May 1932, No 4 Wing ceased to exist, until under the RAF expansion scheme, it reappeared in January 1936.

In 1935, however, the 31st and 32nd entries together totalled some 1,500 apprentices. In August 1936, with the creation of No 3 Wing there were now four apprentice wings at Halton until July 1937 when No 5(A) Wing was formed. In August 1938 it became an airmen's wing when the apprentices were either transferred to RAF Cosford or to the existing apprentice wings.

A member of the 24th Entry, H Rawlinson (mentioned above) described how as one of the 300 successful candidates of more than one thousand that had sat the entrance examination, they had entrained at Baker Street station in London for Wendover in August 1931. They were escorted by a flight lieutenant resplendent in white shirt and collar, turn-ups on his trousers, and carrying a regulation yellow-cane walking stick.

On arrival at Wendover station, seated on wooden forms installed in RAF three-ton trucks equipped with solid rubber tyres, they were uncomfortably bounced up to Bulbeck Barracks at Halton Camp. After alighting from the trucks by the side of the huge parade-ground at No 2 Wing, they were directed into three six-floor barrack-blocks. The large rooms had a double row of beds under each of which was a wooden box for stowing their kit. Fastened to the wall above each bed was a metal locker with two doors. During the day the two parts of their MacDonald beds, 'sprung' with thin metal slats, were telescoped together. The five blankets with interspersed calico sheets, folded into sandwich form, had to be 'squared' on top of the three stacked mattresses.

The next morning only 250 of the entry passed the stiff medical examination at Station Sick Quarters, those rejected being sent back to their homes. After receiving the King's shilling and being allocated their service number they were separately interviewed in order of merit of their entrance examination to determine which technical course they would follow. Rawlinson who was trained as a metal rigger was assigned to 'A' squadron No 2 Wing and wore a light blue band round his cap with a black celluloid disc backing the badge, as well as the customary four-bladed brass propellor on the left sleeve of his tunic.

Flight Lieutenant Alan Jerrard V.C.
Then, continues Rawlinson, followed three years of marching to the large

training workshops or schools accompanied by a full apprentices' band of bagpipes, drums, fifes and trumpets. They frequently passed Flight Lieutenant [Scruff] Jerrard V.C. at 8 a.m. in the mornings cycling up the hill on his way to his office in 'C' Squadron, No 1 Wing. This must have proved difficult since from 23 January 1929 Wings had been marching eight abreast to and from barracks.

Several amusing stories have been recorded in *The Haltonian* about Flt Lt Jerrard, affectionately nicknamed 'Scruff'. He had been awarded the Victoria Cross on 30 March 1918, having twice engaged larger formations of aircraft and going to the aid of a fellow pilot in difficulties. In the second engagement, with nineteen aircraft in the air against him, he shot down a second enemy plane and then, although wounded, continued to attack the pursuing planes before being driven to the ground in a crash landing.[17]

Flt Lt Jerrard performed better in the air – often in one of Halton's Avro *504's* giving 'air experience' flights to newly joined apprentices – than on the parade-ground. In 1932, as 'C' squadron commander, he had the rare distinction of being checked for a haircut on a ceremonial AOC's parade when following the trumpetted 'General salute' and a short silence 'a voice floated up 'Flt Lt Jarrard – you need a haircut'. On another occasion, during a rehearsal probably for the same AOC's parade, one lengthy command during a complicated drill manoeuvre proved too much for him. After fumbling with the preliminary words of command 'Squadron will . . . Squadron . . . As you were! . . . . Squadron . . . Oh, bugger the squadron – carry on Sar' Major!'. There was also the day when the King's Birthday Parade was held on the aerodrome. Prior to 'C' Squadron marching past the saluting base, after slipping on a cow-pat in the long grass, Jerrard livened up the ceremony and delighted the members of 'C' squadron with his extensive vocabulary of explicit language. After retiring from the Royal Air Force the following year, Jerrard's final parade, this time with full military honours, took place at Lyme Regis in 1968.[18]

Coming back to Rawlinson's initial basic training, this covered the maintenance of aircraft such as the Armstrong Whitworth *Siskins*, Avro *504's*, Bristol *Bulldogs* and Hawker *Harts*. The course on construction and maintenance of flying boats concentrated on the Short *'Mussel'* aircraft.

Rigging of biplanes on major inspection included dismantling and erecting of mainplanes with adjusting of the various tension wires between interplane struts to obtain correct dihedral, incidence and stagger . Later in their training, the aerodrome course included starting of various types of engines, propellor swinging (individual and hand-in-hand) and documentation for aircraft maintenance, including of course the all-important Form 700 or record of airworthiness.

Metallurgy included practical as well as theoretical aspects of heat treatment techniques, included hardening and tempering of steels, annealing and normalising of aluminium alloys, soldering and welding techniques, and anodic and other anti-corrosive metal treatments. Inspection and maintenance of aircraft components covered major and minor repairs, and fabric covering, doping and repairs to mainplanes and control surfaces.

In August 1933 Lord Trenchard inspected the 22nd Entry. This was an unusual entry in that of the original 481 Halton apprentices, 8 had purchased their discharge, 21 were discharged as 'unlikely to become efficient airmen', 9 were discharged on medical grounds, 4 had died, 12 were put back to junior entries, and 14 had been transferred from senior entries leaving 438 to pass out from Halton. By contrast, no less than 90% of the Entry were classified as either LAC's (69) or AC1's – the highest percentage in the history of Halton. Another all-time best was Sgt App A. J. Mason's exceptional results of 90% in the educational examination and 91% at the Central Trade Test Board which earned him the Elliott Memorial Prize and a Lord Wakefield Scholarship with a cadetship to Cranwell (accompanied by three other apprentices) where on graduation he was awarded three prizes.

During the years between 1920 and 1934 the Air Force was 'the Cinderella of the Forces of the Crown', a period during which Trenchard had to resist those who resented an independent air service. Moreover, defence spending on all three services had had to take second place to restoring the war savaged economy. As Air Chief Marshal Sir Michael Armitage has pointed out much of the credit for enhancing the standing of the RAF was due to Trenchard. In this way, events such as The Hendon Air Pageant first held in 1920, entries in the Schneider Cup Race and the long-range flights of the late 'twenties, sports, gymnastic displays and the introduction of bands all served to improve the public image of the Royal Air Force.[19]

For more than a dozen years after the First World War, expenditure on the armed forces assumed that no major war was to be expected within ten years. But in 1932, following the unexpected attack by Japan on Shanghai, the British Government cancelled the 'ten-year rule'. The economic crisis facing the world and disarmament under discussion in Geneva ruled out any question of rearmament. The position changed only at the end of 1933 when the work of the Disarmament Conference had proved to be ineffective and Adolph Hitler had begun to rattle his sabre in Germany. As a result, a series of expansion schemes increased the projected size of the Royal Air Force with Bomber and Fighter Commands replacing the old commands known as Air Defence of Great Britain, Bombing Area, and Fighting Area.[20]

Expansion and Boy Entrants

Increased requirements for additional aircrew and ground staff were reflected in the annual air estimates. In this way for example, the 1935 *Air Estimates* increased the number of airmen pilots from 250 to a figure of 540 while the yearly entry of boys for training as aircraft apprentices was brought up from a pre-expansion figure of 550 to over 1,000. A new class of 'Boy Entrant' was introduced for the trades of armourer, wireless operator and photographer. Although requiring a good standard of education, the level of mechanical knowledge and education was lower than that called for from aircraft apprentices. The boy entrants, whose training lasted for about one year, were mainly selected by interview from unsuccessful candidates in the apprenticeship examination to serve for a shorter period of service. In this way, between 1934 and August 1939 about 4,000 boy entrants were entered. A new type of air observer recruited from the apprentices and boy entrants was introduced.

Rearmament led to the construction of eight new barrack-blocks for Paine Wing. In January 1935 the intake of the 31st Entry had increased to 551 apprentices. This trend continued in August with the 32nd Entry of 916 apprentices and again in August 1936 with the 1,250 intake of the 34th Entry.[21]

By 1936 the accelerated expansion of the Royal Air Force, announced in May the previous year, meant that 2,500 pilots and 22,000 airmen had to be trained in less than two years. Again the *Air Estimates* in 1937 refer to expansion of the RAF to a total of 70,000 exclusive of those personnel serving on the Indian establishment. In addition, the continued support by Headmasters, Local Education Authorities and others concerned of the opportunities open in the Air Force, and of the needs of the country in air defence, would be required to meeet the large demands which lay ahead.

Meanwhile at Halton, in July 1936, the results of the 28th Entry were encouraging. Of the 169 apprentices passing out, there were 4 cadetships, 13 LAC's, 140 AC1's and 16 AC2's. This was the first entry to have its revision period conducted in a separate section of the workshops under specially selected instructors. Apprentices were thus enabled to refresh their knowledge acquired over their three-year period of training as well as acquainting themselves with the maintenance of aircraft and other duties awaiting them when posted to their units.[22]

In his printed reply to a question in the House of Commons at the end of 1936, the Minister for the Co-ordination of Defence, Sir Thomas Inskip, gave the following figures for the recruitment of apprentices and boys in the three services:

	1930/1	1931/2	1932/3	1933/4	1934/5	1935/6	1936/7
Royal Navy a)	163	165	174	166	195	225	267(d)
Army (b)	474	294	471	427	449	529	200(e)l
RAF (c)	1,121	902	508	582	899	2,063	2,725(f)

(a) Age limits 15-16 years	(d) 1 April 1936 to 2.12.1936
(b) Age limits 14-16 years	(e) 1 October 1936 to 2.12.1936
(c) Age limits 15-17 years	(f) 1 January 1936 to 2.12.1936

Floggings at Halton

In Britain corporal punishment is now happily a thing of the past – some might say merely a painful memory. But particularly in pre-war years, floggings at most public and grammar schools was an accepted form of punishment. In his *History of the Rod*, the Rev W M Cooper recounts that in the Navy in 1854, a circular on punishments authorised the use of the cane on the hand to check inattention or dirty habits in boys, but there is no doubt that this rule was liberally interpreted. In 1858 special regulations were issued for the flogging of naval cadets ' using a birch rod as in public schools', with a maximum of 24 strokes. In 1867 flogging in the British Army was abolished. Nevertheless, in Scotland alone, in a written reply to a questioner it was recorded in *Hansard* (3.11.1937) that 230 juveniles under the age of 16 had been birched during the year 1937.

At Halton a recent enquiry among ex-apprentices has revealed that between October 1925 and 1938 there were about ten instances of public canings at Halton. In a personal letter Wg Cdr Kimber assured me that he had witnessed one such incident in 1931 along with 999 other apprentices, and it was something he could never forget.

It appears that this type of punishment was awarded usually for instances of theft and then only after prior permission had been officially obtained from the apprentice's parents. With the apprentices, officers and nco's forming a three-sided square, and in the presence of the commanding officer and adjutant, the apprentice who had been found guilty of theft clad in gymn shorts, was marched on to the parade-ground. There, after first being spread-eagled over a vaulting horse by four SP's (RAF service policemen) a warrant officer SP administered 12 strokes with a long cane. A medical officer accompanied by two orderlies examined the boy's face and shorts after each stroke. Kimber recounts that apart from the swish of the cane there was complete silence from those present. It later transpired that the apprentice, later officially cleared, had taken the blame to shield an LAC airman, with a family, who was subsequently reduced to AC2. The apprentice on leaving Halton became a pilot and was killed during the war.[24]

Group Captain T G Mahaddie DSO, DFC, AFC (all three decorations together with the Czech Military Cross were awarded in February 1943) and also a member of the 17th Entry, recalled a similar episode at about the same period. It appears that a dozen apprentices had clubbed together to purchase a large American car. To 'hot-up' the dashboard of their unauthorised transport, they borrowed 'on long loan' several obsolete instruments from the instrument panel of a long abandoned aeroplane, probably a Boulton Paul *Sidestrand*, that had weathered several winters on the airfield.

During a search the instrument taken by one member of the syndicate was discovered, Mahaddie meanwhile had disposed of his part, an ancient altimeter, of the now hot property. He had first suspended it by a string from the barrack-room window. Later after concealing it beneath a towel around his neck during

Group Captain T G Mahaddie, DSO, DFC, AFC, C Eng, AFRAeS.
(Photo via HAAA)

one of his practice cross-country runs he buried it in the woods beneath one of Halton's beeches. The apprehended apprentice, who refused to give the names of the other members of the syndicate, was sentenced to be flogged. He remained adamnant that there was no point in a dozen apprentices also being flogged.

About 600 members of the Wing formed up on the square to witness the caning by a burly flight sergeant policeman. Mahaddie, who says he felt every one of the strokes, considered that never even in his operational career had he met anyone braver than this particular apprentice. Mahaddie wondered whether one day someone roving in the forests with a metal detector will be mystified to discover his ancient altimeter buried beneath the fallen leaves.[25]

The same punishment was witnessed in 1935 when the 'crime' on this occasion was borrowing a bicycle-lamp without the owner's permission – a fairly frequent occurrence among cycle owners at pre-war Halton. Again a hollow square was formed by the three squadrons of the 33rd Entry, but this time the apprentice was firmly held on a trestle-table by two Service Policemen. While six strokes were laid on with considerable force by the flight sergeant 'snoop', a continuous growl went up from the assembled apprentices who, it seems, were on the point of breaking ranks. Throughout that day the apprentices in No 4 Wing, shocked by this public punishment, ate their meals and went about their duties in complete silence. The 'criminal' on leaving Halton was later commissioned.[26]

Another caning took place in the early months of 1937. The whole of No 4 Wing were formed up in a hollow square on the fourth side of which stood a trestle table. According to the 35th Entry apprentice who witnessed this not long after arriving at Halton, the only result of such Draconian measures was an uncomfortable, sullen silence among the assembled ranks of apprentices.[27]

Certainly from 1939 onwards there were no more canings at Halton. Punishments continued to consist of extra fatigues. The award for anything more serious such as smoking – always a capital offence before the age of 18 , subsequently reduced to $17\frac{1}{2}$ – resulted in Form 252 action. An offender could expect to receive from his flight commander a sentence of between 3 to 14 days C.C. (confined to camp), depending on the number of occasions he had sinned. Those punished wore a yellow band on their arm to denote that they were undergoing 'jankers'. These 'janker-wallahs' continued with their normal routine at schools or workshop training as well as attending extra parades and doing fatigues.

Wg Cdr Kimber recalled two apprentices, both intelligent and likable characters, who by about 1928 had each accumulated not less than 500 days' jankers at Halton. They had opted for a life of 'crime' with a view to obtaining their discharge, but as long as their offences remained of a minor nature the authorities, undoubtedly alerted to the strategy, tactfully refrained from intervening.[28]

The first Headmaster at Cranwell and Halton

A history of Halton would not be complete without further mention of Lt Col AFS Caldwell CBE DSO, a senior member of the RAF Education Service. He was educated at Worcester and Trinity College, Dublin where he was a Senior Moderator in mathematics. At an early age he subsequently became Headmaster of Daventry Grammar School and then Headmaster of Sligo Grammar School. A keen sportsman, he played football for Dublin University, hockey for Northamptonshire and Devonshire and cricket for Worcestershire.

Coming direct from his battalion in Ireland, Caldwell taught the first entry at the Boys' Wing Cranwell when in Febrary 1920 he was appointed Headmaster at the Boys' Wing Cranwell. After organizing this school for Boy Mechanics where he remained for nearly two years, in 1922 he was moved to Halton where he organized and reconstructed the existing schools. He became Principal of the School in October 1926 and remained at Halton until his departure from the Service in 1932.

An outstanding personality, during his Cranwell service Caldwell was known for his stern rebuffs 'but the offender was always comforted five minutes later by some merry joke'. On his departure from Halton as Principal Education

Officer, by his leadership he had created a tradition of demanding absolute loyalty while in return giving unswerving support to the men he led. The editor of *The Halton Magazine* commented 'only to those actually serving are known the hardships and disppointments of those early days . . . In the case of great men of the world, a cool calculating selfishness is too often apparent. In Colonel Caldwell such a trait was totally absent, and missing worldly greatness on this account, he became great in the truest sense of the word'.

Caldwell was succeeded by H A Cox OBE MA, who had joined Halton from Oundle School in August 1926. During the period 1937 to 1939 (see *Air Force Lists* 1937/1939) the Principal Education Officer at Halton was Adam H Robson MC MSc PhD. Following the expansion at Halton, by 1937 Cox headed the No 1 Wing educational staff but as at January 1939 his name was no longer shown on the strength.[29]

NOTES

5 The peaceful years (1927-1936)

1   *Flight* 20.1.1927
2   *ibid,* 19.1.1927, 3.2.1927
3   *The Halton Magazine*, Easter 1927
4   *Daily Telegraph, 30.3.1990*
5   *The Scout,* 11.6.1927
6   *The Haltonian,* Summer 1984
7   Personal letter (Freddy Joyce 61st Entry Ruislip)
      NOTE Service numbers allocated to Apprentice Clerks at Ruislip were 590001-592080
8   H Rawlinson MS, RAF Museum
9   Spencer Smith, 'Call Back Yesterday'
10   Kimber, op cit, pp 63,67-70
11   *The Haltonian,* Summer 1991 (A. L. Holland)
12   *ibid,* Summer 1983 (Walter R. Pearce)
13   *ibid,* Winter 1988 (P Levy); Adam op cit ; AHB
14   *Flight* 2.8.1928; *The Haltonian,* Summer 1982
15   *ibid,* 10.5.1928
16   *ibid,* 11.4.1930
      NOTE – The Columbia Gramophone Society recorded three of these songs
17   *The Haltonian,* Summer 1982
18   *ibid,* Summer 1982 (Mr Wilson); *ibid,* Autumn 1983 (E J Bunting), *ibid,* Summer 1984 (E Balkwill)
19   Armitage, op cit
20   Basil Collier, *Leader of the Few,* London, 1957, pp 143, 144

21 Armitage, op cit
22 *The Aeroplane*, 5.8.1936
23 *Hansard*, 2.12.1936
24 Kimber, op cit, pp 65,66 : *The Haltonian*, Summer 1987 (E. J. Bunting)
25 Gp Capt T. G. Mahaddie, *Hamish*, 1989
    NOTE The LAA in charge of Mahaddie's room 13-14 was Neville Sparks
    who passed out LAC, and whose father was editor of *Flight*. This fact may
    well explain the considerable interest shown in Halton by *Flight*
    (Typescript 'The Fledgeling' by 562270, AHB)
26 *The Haltonian*, Winter 1989 ('Skull' Thompson)
27 *ibid,* Summer 1990 (Syd Clay)
28 Kimber, op cit, pp 42,43
29 *Boys' Wing Magazine*, Spring 1922 (First number); *The Halton Magazine*,
    Summer 1932; Haslam, op cit, p 45

Chapter Six

YEARS OF EXPANSION (1937-1940)

The Royal Air Force remained a small but highly professional corps d'élite until 1935 when Britain began to build up her defences. But it was necessary for Hitler to march into Vienna in March 1938 before decisive action was taken to meet the Nazi threat. Time was then running short and emergency steps had to be taken to prepare for a war now regarded as inevitable.

One measure taken to attract recruits was to modernize uniforms which apart from the colour had remained the same as those worn during Boer War days. As a result in September 1936 dress regulations changed for the first time since the formation of the RAF in 1918. Uniforms, which had changed in 1919 from khaki to blue, now included blue collars and ties for all ranks, and under *AMO* A 93 (30.4.1936) breeches and puttees, were replaced by slacks. Officers ceased to carry a walking stick and airmen their hated little RAF-crested canes. Soft glengarries, RFC-type headwear (officially field-service caps), were reintroduced for all ranks.[1]

Hundreds of pairs of the now obsolete puttees (usually described as horse-bandages) were tied together to form enormous chains slung across the parade ground between the barrack-blocks. The bell-type greatcoats, cut in British-warm style to match 'winged' breeches, were withdrawn and issued to new apprentices as 'seconds' for everyday wear. The nickle-plated crested-knob canes, hitherto an essential part of an airman's uniform, were discarded since nobody wanted these, invariably dented, 'tooth-picks' even as a souvenir.

All leading newspapers and aviation weeklies, under the heading 'Why not make it the Royal Air Force', announced the 1937 recruitment needs of the expanding Royal Air Force. As well as 1,500 pilots, 1,500 'well-educated boys of secondary school standard' were required as aircraft apprentices to become fitters, wireless operator mechanics, instrument makers or fitter armourers. In addition to Apprentice Clerks, there was a need for Boy Entrants for training as wireless operators, armourers or photographers, and 11,000 airmen for various ground trades.

A total of 1,911 candidates from all over Britain (including myself) sat the apprentice entrance examination in June. The pass list appeared in *The Times*, which regularly carried news items on the aircraft apprentice scheme (see Bibliography). In this way, for example, it reported Parents' Day in 1938 as well as a full account with photographs of George VI's visit in April 1939.

During August and September 1937, three intakes of 'sprog' members of the 36th Entry, on arrival at nearby Wendover Station travelled in hired coaches for the two-mile drive up to the parade ground of Maitland Barracks. For the remainder of the three-year stay at Halton, despite suitcases, the journey to and from Wendover was made by foot.

After departure of the wireless, electrical and instrument-maker apprentices for training at Cranwell, the remaining one thousand new entrants of the 36th Entry, including 100 prospective armourers, were assigned for training on airframes or engines, respectively, either to Nos 1 or 2 Wings located in Henderson and Grove Barracks. The five other entries under training at Halton included the senior 31st and 32nd. The 36th Entry arrivals were first directed for a short stay to the well-equipped No 5 Wing (Shepperds Barracks), complete with spring beds and wardrobe-type lockers, pending its reallocation as an airmens' Wing.[2]

B Squadron, No 1 Wing, 36th Entry, August 1939. Gas masks carried. Author in centre, second rank, on right of Flt Lt Warrington.

New arrivals at Halton never failed to be impressed by the magnificence of the beech woods covering the rising ground in the hills at the back of the camp. Beautiful in summer and autumn when they formed a green or golden belt about the red-brick buildings, in winter, with the wind howling through the branches, they assumed a sinister appearance.

An unsurmountable barrier of spiked-palings (long ago removed) around No 1 Wing ensured that apprentices left the Camp via the Guardroom entrance. An unofficial exit, however, had been contrived by members of the 24th Entry in the early 'thirties. The lower rivet securing one of the unsurmountable palings to the lower cross-bar had been removed. In this way, the paling pivotted freely on its upper rivet. Meanwhile, the rivet heads, minus the sawn-off shank, were carefully replaced on each side of the paling thus leaving it to swing naturally back to the vertical position. The exit, strategically positioned, formed a convenient escape-path up the grassy slopes and away into the woods and the road leading to Tring.[3]

But to return to the 36th Entry, new entrants still in civilian clothes paraded in No 4 Wing NAAFI for attestation by a squadron leader where they repeated the solemn Oath of Allegiance to His Majesty George VI and his Successors. Following the issue of uniforms and on completion of one week's drilling the entry moved over to the older No 1 or 2 Wing buildings.

Then followed a further week of square-bashing. There were of course apprentices who could not make it, ranging from the unusually dim to those who could not stand discipline. This probably inspired one apprentice poet in the *Halton Magazine* of Xmas 1937 to write:

DID YOU KNOW MUFF ?

For a rookie A. A. Muff
Is exceptionally tough.
E.O.'s blink at him and stare,
Sergeants stamp around and swear,
And discuss with faces grim
What on earth to do with him.

German Air Force Mission visits Halton

Barely two months after arrival at Halton, we learned that the heads of the German Air Force had been invited by the Government – despite the vigorous protests of Winston Churchill, who nevertheless met the mission at a dinner given by Lord Trenchard – to visit several RAF stations. This visit to Halton was in return for that of the RAF to the German Air Force earlier that year.

During their week's stay in England the German Mission met the heads of the Royal Air Force including the CAS (ACM Sir Cyril Newall), AOC Fighter Command (ACM Sir Hugh Dowding),

AOC Bomber Command (ACM Sir Edgar Ludlow-Hewitt) as well as MRAF Lord Trenchard and Lord Swinton (Secretary of State for Air). Swinton who is mentioned in the German Mission's report as "following that trend in the Cabinet which favours an understanding with Germany" was dismissed in May 1938.

An Air Staff Note circulated to the Station Commanders concerned included Air Commodore Reid as AOC Halton. The personal note to him from Headquarters No 24 (Training Group), also at Halton, asked Reid to cancel afternoon tea from his draft programme for the German visit which would end at 15.30 h. The Nazi flag was not be flown, but as a compliment to the German Air

Force small Nazi emblems (to be obtained via the British Air Attaché Berlin) were to be displayed on luncheon tables. It was desired to impress the German Mission with the RAF's state of preparedness and efficiency 'to counteract the impression which various visitors to Germany of the milksop and defeatist variety have given the German authorities – namely that we are unprepared for any sort of emergency which cannot be met by paper and palaver'. As the CAS considered that General Milch would be looking for evidence of physical fitness the Mission might be allowed to see (as it were casually) apprentices at physical training. A list of defence points that should not be mentioned was attached, but under the heading 'Training' it was noted 'we have nothing to hide'.

Lord Swinton welcomes the German Mission to the Air Ministry. The party, which included the German Air Minister, General Milch (centre), General-Lieutenant Stumpf and General-Major Ernst Udet (left), visited RAF Halton on 21 October 1937.
(*The Illustrated London News* Picture Library.)

The agenda included visits to several RAF stations and even Buckingham Palace where King George VI received the members of the German Mission. Their final visit was to RAF Halton on 21st October 1937, when Air Marshal Sir Charles Burnett the AOC-in-Chief Training Command officially welcomed the Germans with a Guard of Honour made up of apprentices from No 1 Wing. During his inspection of 'the seat of all that is latest in education', as *The Aeroplane* put it, 'General Udet renewed joyfully his acquaintance with the Bristol *Fighter*, of which a fine specimen was on view'.

On the return to barracks at mid-day, the four Apprentice Wings marched past the much-decorated General Erhard Milch, Secretary of State for Air, who took the salute, Lt Gen Stumpff, Chief of the Air Staff, Maj-Gen Udet, Chief of the Technical Staff who had downed 62 British planes, as well as the German Air Attaché.

A second march-past was arranged for the benefit of General Milch who stood almost alone to take the salute on the main road leading from the workshops. This was unrehearsed and we apprentices duly marched past in shirt-sleeve order with overalls 'neatly rolled' under left arms. Even at this juncture members of the German Air Force could hardly be regarded as friends and it is odd that only two years later we were at war ! One apprentice while marching past had a 'Baby Ensign' camera concealed in his left hand and managed to take a reasonable shot of the Germans. Pat Biegal (35th) who recalled this incident, says that the lunch served that day in No 3 Wing – which evoked a '*Gut, gut*' from a beaming Udet – bore no resemblance to their usual fare.

At a press conference a few days later General Milch spoke well of what they had seen at Halton and their "good impression of the rising generation" and "the large number of sporting facilities".

The visit of the German Mission included one bomber and two fighter stations (Mildenhall, Odiham and Hornchurch) as well as the Cadet College at Cranwell. After inspecting two squadrons of Gloster *Gladiators*, the German Air Attaché's report commented on the "good turn-out and obviously excellent morale of the fighter pilots" and added that "*Spitfires* etc, have not yet been delivered". Following a flying display by the cadets, the reception arranged at Cranwell included a typical air force "Dining-in Night" with the orchestra playing German marches and airs. The usual after-dinner games in the Mess played by the younger officers were much appreciated by the German guests!

The guest-night, also reported in *The Aeroplane*, for some of the Germans must have been 'a shattering experience'. Several of the younger RAF officers present had demonstrated '*Moriarty*'- where two blindfolded opponents in full mess-kit and flat out on the carpet, endeavour to home-in (sometimes with a resultant bloody nose) on the other's head with a heavy rolled-up *Tatler*, while their free left hands remain clasped together. The report ended that the guests had survived the Air Force hospitality.[4]

The officers

The officers in the four, and later five, wings (named Henderson, Grove, Maitland, Shepperd and subsequently Paine) at Halton had little to do in the way of administrative work. To maintain their aircrew status they had only to fly four hours a month and "flips" to sports meetings or receptions at other RAF stations were conveniently "laid on". Promotion was almost unheard of and flight lieutenants often soldiered on for as long as twelve years.

On Army lines, the officers' mess had separate dining arrangements for senior and junior officers. Calling and card-leaving were part of the social round. Of the eighty-or-so officers, those who lived-in dined in full mess-kit, except at weekends when they relaxed in dinner jackets. Despite all the grandeur, junior officers, like most apprentices, found it difficult to obtain a hot bath. While standards of dress and etiquette were maintained at the highest level, mess parties usually ended with the dangerous sport of sledging down the carpetted double-width stairway in the dinner-gong, a tradition that had originated in 1925 and is still observed on, and only on, official guest nights.[5]

Except for those few occasionally required to sound trumpet-fanfares from the balcony, apprentices remained blissfully unaware of this golden era for their officers. Ten years afterwards, Group Captain A J Nicholas, OBE, a junior engineer officer at Halton, whom I remembered as "Titch", told me how he had been reprimanded by the Commanding Officer for failing to sign the WARNING OUT book in the mess sufficiently frequently. He was expected to absent himself from Halton attending to his social functions at least twice weekly! Drinks could only be obtained from waiters who attended to orders from the ante-room; fortunately for his pocket, as a married officer Nicholas lived out and only dined in mess on compulsory dining-in nights. In 1937 additional officers were required to supervise the flood of apprentices brought in under the expansion scheme. At that date a three-storey block housing forty officers was constructed as an annex to Halton House.

Selected ex-World War I officers were invited in 1937 to rejoin as reserve (Class CC) officers. One of these flight commanders, Sdn Ldr [Major] C M Crowe, MC, DFC, a Royal Flying Corps fighter-ace had served with No 56 Squadron from its first days in France. While attacking a German Albatros, Crowe had had his goggles shot from his flying helmet. He flew with Captain Ball VC, DSO, on his last flight when he was shot down by the brother of the ruthless Baron von Richthofen – "the jolly old Baron" as he was known in the RFC. Crowe's dogfights are described in Captain Albert Ball's biography which I loaned to most rooms of our block in 1 Wing.[6]

I ran into Crowe on two occasions after Halton. The first in 1948 at Manston, the former Battle of Britain fighter station. He was then still in uniform but held an Air Training Corps post in the area. The second time was in 1956, at Vickers-Armstrongs (Aircraft) Weybridge which I had joined the previous year after opting for retirement from the RAF to become Personal Assistant to the Chief Engineer. Seated in the Design Office – which unbelievedly housed some 700 designers and draughtsmen in one enormous hall – was my former commanding officer, now bespectacled, leaning over a desk updating aircraft specifications. My boss had no idea he had an ex-RFC fighter ace on his staff, and I was instrumental in getting him transferred to a rather more interesting post.

His replacement in 'C' Squadron, Flt Lt Wallington, RAFO, complete with big teddy-bear overcoat and large Talbot, had played a bearded German U-boat commander in the film 'Q-Boats'. For the Halton show produced by the apprentices in 1939, he persuaded an attractive starlet friend then appearing in a West End show to join the cast on stage.

The daily routine

Following a long tradition, shortly after arrival at Halton all apprentices received their aerial baptism. In this way, new arrivals after being issued with parachutes and helmets made their first flight, generally in an Avro *Tutor*. My earliest recollection of No 1 Wing was watching a squad of tough looking senior-entry apprentices doubling onto the square for pre-breakfast physical jerks. One or two shouted 'Don't forget the trial period !' this was in reference to the first three-months' service when an apprentice could claim discharge as a right on payment of £20. After the trumpetted 'Rouse', five minutes before the 6.30 a.m. reveille, the duty messcooks collected in white buckets our 'gunfire' consisting of tea and teeth-breaking Osborne biscuits. Then came Reveille when the 'MacDonald' beds had to be telescoped shut and blankets neatly folded.

Led by a physical training instructor, clad in blue-and-black ringed vest with tight navy-blue trousers, apprentices doubled to the barrack square for the morning warm-up. Barely thirty minutes remained to shower – when there was hot water – change and prepare for the morning parade. I enjoyed these early morning canters and presumably for that reason was later selected for the Wing team in the annual physical training competition.

Each morning the orderly officer's instructions for the dress of the day – which in rainy weather meant either wearing or carrying black oilskins – were communicated by the duty trumpeter. Before the parade, at each landing of the block in response to an NCO's repeated shout 'Any coughs, colds, sore-throats or headaches ?' suffering apprentices put their names down for sick-parade.

Apprentices then formed up on the parade ground. There, after the order 'Roman Catholics and Jews fall out' – very few did – and a three-ringed padré had chanted his piece, the Wings marched down the hill to either schools or workshops to the skirl of the pipes or the blare of calvary trumpets.

Life was uneventful, and since apprentices had to be back in barracks by 21.00 they were virtually confined to camp. This made no real difference since the nearest towns Tring and Aylesbury were several miles away and buses were infrequent. In any case, few apprentices had enough money even for a visit to a cinema. During my stay at Halton I rarely visited Aylesbury and cannot recall having been to Tring.

Education at Halton

Training at schools and workshops was intensive. The more than forty education officers were all civilians (see Appendix J). These included bespectacled Tommy Hampson, Editor of the *Halton Magazine* who after obtaining his Running Blue at Oxford in 1929 went on to gain the 800m world record at Los Angeles three years later; A. H. Woolcock, goalkeeper for the amateur English team, with his rich wardrobe of Harris and Cheviot tweed suits, and who in 1940 as a flying officer was killed at Dunkirk. They both taught general studies, including military geography. In the summer of 1939 in reply to my question about promotion prospects for apprentices, Woolcock confided that about one-third of the apprentices were considered immediately suitable for commissioned rank. There was also little Mr Pinder, who tried to teach us the calculus, and softly spoken Mr Dawson who taught engineering drawing and who apparently finished up in Malta. Others of these well-qualified officers – many of whom donned uniform during the war – taught electricity, aerodynamics, the new-fangled hydraulics, mathematics, properties and strengths of materials, metallurgy and even something about Claudel Hobson carburretors and sophisticated magneto systems.

The educational climate at Halton caused one apprentice-poet to erupt in the following lines published anonymously pre-war in the *Halton Magazine*:

> I love the School – it's studious quiet
> Delights me more and more:
> I love to learn the Calculus
> Or else the Civil War.
> I love to learn to draw a point,
> To know why heat is warm:
> I love the window where the sun
> Comes peeping in at morn.
>
> Walking along the corridors
> I meditate on Fate;
> Although such meditations
> Incline to make me late.
> And when I'm reprimanded
> By Masters I adore;
> I could not love the school so well,
> Loved I not Workshops more.

The Trenchard Library with Apprentices of No 155 (the final Entry) studying for their final examinations.   (Author's Photo.)

Courses at Halton covered every aspect of aeronautical engineering and the thorough instruction followed by written tests provided an excellent basis for more advanced studies either in the service or for the many who went on to obtain university-level qualifications for membership of the engineering institutions or the Royal Aeronautical Society.

The Intermediate Examination in December 1937 for General Studies, a printed paper, set for apprentices who had been at Halton for only one year included the following questions:

– *To what reasons do you ascribe the development of national socialism (the Nazi movement) in Germany?*

– *Describe the aims of French foreign policy since the war.*

– *Describe the system of state planning for industry and agriculture practised by the Soviet goverment. Have we anything like it in England?*

– *What do you consider the best piece of characterization you have met in reading any play this year? Describe the points of character that impressed you.*

Not all apprentices profitted from the instruction given by the well-qualified civilian education officers as was reflected in the Summer issue of the *Halton Magazine*:

> Aircraft Apprentice Clarence Mull
> Found his General Studies dull.
> Instead of doing useful work
> On Ibn Saud and Attaturk
> This extraordinary boy
> Drew pictures of Miss Myrna Loy
> And gained reproof from his E.O.
> And you'll agree, quite rightly so.

Meanwhile in the Commons in March 1938, a Mr Hopkinson spoke about opportunities for promotion in the Air Force. He said that in the Army (and the same applied in the Navy), 'if a young subaltern is sent to a regiment they take one good look at him and they can tell from that good look whether he is likely to make an officer or not . . . In the Air Force it often happens that the most unpromising of young officers at first sight turns out to be exactly the sort that is wanted. In the course of my experience . . . I have found case after case of really first-rate junior officers – according to their squadron leaders, who ought to be in a position to judge – who would have been condemned by any decent regiment or any decent ship'.

He said that Air Force officers came from every class and it was not possible to say which schools produced the best. His comments on Halton were interesting:

'That links up with another point with regard to commissions, and that is the commissions given to the aircraftmen trained at that great school Halton. That school has been run by a series of enthusiasts who are very able men indeed. It is a magnificent school, and the education and the training which the boys get there are as good as they get at any of the best public schools in the country. The result is that a considerable proportion of the boys who pass out of Halton are really qualified to take commissions, and there is, I know, in the minds of some of the senior officers, a strong feeling that Halton boys ought to have rather more commissions open to them than is the case at the present time....I have come across a considerable number of those boys who are fit to have commissions and ought to be given better opportunities of obtaining them. I know the present position is partly due to the fact that they cannot be spared from their present duties, but Halton itself must be enlarged in course of time, and I hope that it will be . . .' [7]

Workshops training

The several hundred Workshop instructors, mainly ex-RAF or ex-RFC, were patient, kind but effective. Workshops training for many generations of apprentices included 'basic' metalwork. Exercise No 1 consisted of reducing with hammer and cold chisel the overall dimensions of a 4-inch side steel block gripped firmly in a bench-vice. The noise created by a hundred hammers on shuddering benches made speech impossible while countless bandaged thumbs, including my own, testified to the doubtful utility of this exercise. I was surprized recently to learn that this anvil-bashing had been criticized as early as 1926 when it was recommended to machine three of the four faces of the block (see Appendix D: Education and training).

For most apprentices this was the first and only occasion they would be called upon to use a cold chisel!

The heat-treatment course in Workshops covered all types of steels and light alloys, while at School we learned all about corresponding eutectics and eutectoids. One practical exercise was for each apprentice to harden and temper the cold chisel referred to above. A later exercise, was to manufacture a pair of bending-bars, having different radii, for gripping mild steel or duralumin sheet prior to shaping. The final test exercise was to fashion a tee-shaped male insert and its matching female frame.

With the introduction of new engines and aircraft it became clear that the three-year training period would be too short. When the decision came to divide the engines/airframe training into two separate courses the 36th Entry had already completed the preliminary engines course. One afternoon Mr Gomme, our engines'intructor, exploded when following reassembly and valve-timing, the *Gypsy VI* in-line engine, immediately on being started clanked to a standstill. His shouted protests on the tarmac could be heard even above the unusual noises emerging from the belching exhausts. He was even more unhappy when on removal of the cylinder-head a 2-inch bolt was extracted from the depths of a much-scored cylinder.

The transition to all-metal aircraft caused problems for instructing staff. The problem was the lack of new aircraft and experienced instructors whose skills were required in the aircraft factories now short of manpower. Preliminary rigging still included removal and reassembly of the mainplanes of ancient Avro *504K*'s. The training we had received to adjust flying, landing and incidence wires against clinometer readings to obtain correct dihedral and incidence angles, although essential for the rigging of biplanes, did not help when removing or assembling the wings of larger aircraft such as the *Battle* and *Wellington*, etc.

A short carpentry course was sufficient to enable apprentices to repair wooden aircraft such as Avro *Ansons*, Airspeed *Oxfords*, etc. A soldering and welding course gave an insight into this specialized and difficult branch of engineering.

Early in 1939, a pair of *Spitfires* made their appearance in the workshops. A two-week course on these then top-secret fighters was given by two young corporal instructors, still bronzed from their recent tour in Australia. They solemnly instructed on the importance of weighing all materials used in repairing the fabric-covered control surfaces. This was to calculate the mass balancing necessary about the hinge-lines for ensuring aerodynamic equilibrium. It is difficult to imagine ground staff one year later sitting down with paper and pencil to calculate moments prior to repairing bullet-holes in elevators or ailerons.

The courses covered so many different components of various aircraft, such as brakes, undercarriages, fuel systems, controls, etc, that a stage was reached when apprentices could almost intuitively understand the functioning of a particular component with minimum instruction. This aspect of Halton training was to prove invaluable on operational stations when quick turnrounds were the key factor in keeping aircraft flying and where instructional manuals did not exist.

The six-week aerodrome course on aircraft such as the Bristol *Blenheim*, Fairey *Battle* (notorious for poor performance and inferior armament) *Lysanders*, and the geodetically designed Vickers *Wellesley* bomber of basket-weave construction intended to take punishment as well as providing extra tankage and storage space. Starting engines of all kinds included prop' swinging with the never-to-be-forgotten 'switches off, petrol on, suck-in' followed by 'switches on, contact'. Larger aircraft engines involved several apprentices holding hands to drag clear the one who handled the propellor. Starting a Hawker *Hart* by hand called for smaller apprentices to balance precariously on one wheel while turning the starting handle inserted in the engine cowling.

Theoretical and practical instruction continued on various hydraulically and pneumatically operated control systems and undercarriages as well as maintenance and repair schemes for the all-metal stressed skin construction of the "modern" aircraft. Training on the latter aircraft was not, however, always realistic. For example, to inspect the main-spars of *Battles*, a score of Parker-Kalon screws securing leading edge panels to the wing had to be removed. In operational service, however, either the screwheads would shear off, and require a dental operation to remove the root, or had disappeared under numerous coatings of enamel. The problem was often removing other chaps' sheared screw-shanks, or chipping through layers of case-hardened paint to locate screwheads. There is no doubt that during 1940, *Battle* main-spars over a wide front received minimum attention !

One event recorded in my diary (see Appendix C) was when the Boer War Memorial was struck by lightning during the night of 29th January 1939. This fact is recorded for posterity on the now rebuilt Memorial on Coombe Hill, still a well-known landmark in the Halton area.[8]

'Specially selected' disciplinary NCO's

The silent 'h's' and interplay of 'was's' and 'were's' of the well-meaning Group V (aircrafthand) NCO's were lampooned in the twice-yearly *Halton Magazine*. Most of these NCO's, apart from the Service Police or 'snoops', were kindly chaps who rarely entered the barrack-rooms except during weekly inspections.

There were relatively few NCO's since day-to-day discipline was ensured by members of senior entries selected for their prowess at sports, workshops or schools for promotion to apprentice ranks from "snag" up to sergeant. At a much later period a flight-sergeant apprentice and, briefly, even a warrant officer rank was also created.

The "specially selected" (according to the Air Ministry pamphlet) NCO's included Warrant Officer Collard, a tall hollow-faced old soldier, whose barathea tunic, cut calvalry-style, seemed to reach to his knees. With his back to the RAF Ensign facing the combined Nos 1 and 2 Wings of some 1,500 apprentices, his tremendous 'As you were' or 'Let's hear it..THEN !' – would inevitably be triggered by any drill movement which entailed displacing one foot sideways, forwards or backwards. Rehearsing for the AOC's annual inspection (with two march pasts on Troop-the-Colour lines) everyone on the parade ground – even senior officers – became a target for his criticism. On one occasion during a combined No 1 and 2 Wing drill manoeuvre I still remember his vociferous shout , 'Wing Commander Sugden, will you bring your Wing into line . . . THEN !' No 1 Wing duly came into line.

The No 1 Wing warrant officer, a different type of drill-master, one of the last NCO's to be promoted from WO II rank, preferred the "You there, third file, rear rank . . . No not you, the man next to you! . . . Yes, you! . . .'old your 'ead up, WILL YOU ? By this time, every apprentice on parade had lifted his head. One recent correspondent in the *Halton Magazine* wondered whether anyone remembers the notorious Apprentice Stan Still, who seemed to be bawled-out on almost every parade.[9]

The regular Church parades, three Sundays out of four, entailed a best-blue parade with drums and pipes leading to the various places of worship. The now well-known 'Git yer 'at orf in the 'ouse of Gawd' did in fact originate at Halton, but at the time of the first entry in the early 'twenties.[10] At one point the non-religious sermons of a non-conformist padre drew apprentices from other denominations but as one's confession could not be changed without parental consent they had to be directed back to their own churches.

Meanwhile across the square in No 2 Wing there was Flight Sergeant 'Doggy' D., whose rifle drill included 'Nah then, I don't want nobody to do nuffink until I tells yer', and 'When I say FIX, yer don't FIX. When I says BAYONETS, yo' whips 'em out and whips 'em on!'. Flight Sergeant Johnny K., on the other hand, in the words of the 35th Entry ex-apprentice author, preferred to create a place for himself in a sort of Trinity with his: 'The flight sergeant don't like it, Johnny K. don't like it, and I don't like it!'.[12]

Sex at Halton

One author in the *Halton Magazine* has succinctly described this activity at pre-war Halton – there was none! The official attitude to sex clearly laid down by the Service in 1936 in Paragraph 11 of *Rules for Boy Entrants and Apprentices* left no room for doubt: 'Boy entrants are forbidden to associate with females' – this applied even to those who before leaving Halton might have reached the age of twenty. The rule was apparently infringed one day when an apprentice of the 36th Entry was seen to leave the camp accompanied by a girl. He was challenged at the Guardroom by the Service Policeman who almost charged him with being facetious on being informed that it was not in fact a female but his sister (who happened to be employed in the NAAFI).

By 1940 temptation in the shape of WAAF's began to disturb the imposed celibacy of Halton's inmates. The blocks housing WAAF and later WRAF airwomen were declared no-go areas and during 1949 at least two apprentices lost one of their rare 48-passes for being caught out of bounds. Their punishment would no doubt have been heavier had they not first obtained the appropriate letter from their parents permitting them to have girlfriends and ride motorbikes.[15] As late as 1954, 'girl-permits' were still necessary but the concession for motor-bikes had apparently been withdrawn. As one member of the 70th Entry put it, the one was of no use without the other.

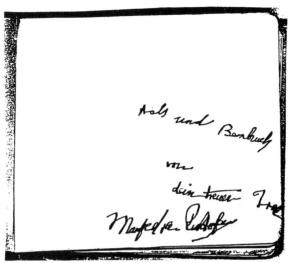

Matters metaphysical – the Red Baron's 'message' received at RAF Halton in 1938. The apprentice writer had no knowledge of German: literally translated it reads 'Break your necks and legs, sincerely Manfred von Richthofen' – a common form of greeting which means 'good luck' or 'all the best'.

(Photo Verlag Ullstein GMBH, Berlin.)

Metaphysical diversions at Halton

During 1936 someone in No 1 Wing became interested in spiritualism. In no time séances were being conducted in the drying-rooms located on each floor of the barrack blocks, or in the small bunks allocated to 'snags' (leading apprentices). Numerous small groups communicated with 'friendly spirits' and obtained messages by various methods. Advanced enthusiasts progressed to automatic writing and some, it was whispered, to medium-conducted séances. One winter evening in 1937, having been invited to join one group I enquired from which area hailed my earliest ancestors. I was surprized to learn 'from the land now covered by the North Sea'.

This unauthorized activity, which had even extended to the Naval Apprentices Wing, an offshoot of No 1 Wing, came to an abrupt end in 1938. One pioneer group, whose meetings took place in the wooded hills behind the Camp, claimed contact with Baron Manfred von Richthofen, the 'Red Knight', who had shot down 80 RFC aircraft. The news spread rapidly with the result that the Church of England chaplain, a squadron leader, asked the leader of the group, an Apprentice of the senior 32nd Entry, to report to his office.

In a recent letter, this ex-apprentice – who with another member of the same group became pilots and were commissioned during the war – has recounted what happened. As he puts it 'Your remarks on the 'psychic phenomena' that swept through No 1 Wing in 1937 bring back old memories after fifty-seven years'. Instead of the dressing down that he expected for these spiritual deviations, the padré, he wrote, 'almost treated me as a colleague – we had a long and interesting discussion on matters metaphysical'.

Not long afterwards, a Wing Routine Order was issued stating that 'the practice of holding séances in No 1 Wing will cease forthwith'. I had long forgotten all this when during his dining-out dinner on his retirement from Headquarters No 63 Group, Chester, in 1951, Gp Capt Nicholas – a pre-war junior officer at Halton – asked me whether I had been there 'during all that hullabaloo over spiritualism in No 1 Wing.' Unfortunately I was unable to pursue the subject further since the next morning he had departed.

Haircutting at Halton

Throughout the long history of Halton one recurring theme in the Halton journals was the question of haircuts. The only alternative to a scalping was a three-mile trudge to Tring at the weekend or to allow one of the enthusiastic amateurs to have a go – with sometimes disastrous results. The civilian barbers at Halton, notorious for their almost surgical operations on apprentice heads, included 'Sweeney Tod', and his shorter colleague, 'Teeny Sod' (alias 'Little Two Thou'). They were presumably related to the sadists 'Clip' and 'Clop' of the earlier 'thirties whose operating time according to Wg Cdr Kimber had been a flat three minutes.

The problem of hair dressing, as far back as 1927, prompted one poet

(Aircraft Apprentice C Apillart) to produce 'Hair-cuts', which appeared in the Easter number of *The Halton Magazine* (first verse only) :

> The chief humiliation the A/A has to bear
> Is to let the Service barber take a cutting of his hair
> The long luxurious tresses that he grows to shade his eyes
> With the barber's sense of beauty do not seem to syn-chronise.

On at least one occasion following the passing out of the Senior Entry, retaliatory action was taken by apprentices. In this way one member of the 35th Entry was retained at Halton for 14 days, after the remainder of his entry had departed, as a guest of the Service Policemen for ensuring that the locks of the No 2 Wing hairdresser also complied with service regulations.[16]

The question of haircuts came to a head, as it were, in 1947 with a mess sit-in at breakfast, started by senior entries, largely in protest against the banning of 'Boston-type' haircuts. A report in the *Daily Mirror*, together with a cartoon showing a recalcitrant apprentice, was accompanied by the following couplet:

> 'O fledgling airmen, the sergeant wonsure
> Hair cut in a more becoming tonsure'.[14]

As a result of all the publicity a senior officer from Air Ministry visited Halton to investigate the grievances. Subsequently the relevant clause in *King's Rules and Regulations* was amended from 'a maximum of one and a half inches on top' to read simply 'neat and tidy'.[15]

An earlier sit-in had occurred at Halton in March 1946 when following a rejection of breakfast the C.O. had ordered a replacement meal. This incident was in fact only one of a series of 'strikes' reflecting discontent at RAF Stations, particularly in the Far East at this time. Causes included slow demobilization, poor food, infrequent mail, lack of recreational activities and of course operational activity.[16]

Similar unrest including mutinies had occurred in the armed forces following the First World War. One effective step taken in 1945 was the setting up of the RAF Educational and Vocational Training Scheme offering the possibility of gaining either the War Certificate or the Forces Preliminary Certificate (University Entrance level). Numbers of instructors were enrolled on RAF stations to teach a variety of subjects for all ranks awaiting demobilisation.

Sports, tree-planting and stone-picking

On sports afternoons the aerodrome area became one enormous sports field where more than fifty games of football, rugby and hockey simultaneously took place. Those who grew tired of walking several miles to the aerodrome and back could take up fencing or swimming, and in the summer tennis.

There was also a small Cyclists' Club, one of the many sections of the Halton Society, organized by one of the civilian instructors. Boxing featured prominently in the sporting activities of Halton. Apprentices were paraded in the large gymnasium for the periodical Barrington Kennet competitions when the officers in mess-dress with white waistcoats and stiff wing-collars occupied ring-side seats.

By the end of 1938 nobody doubted that a full-scale war was imminent. It is not clear who actually issued the order but it was considered that the wide-open spaces surrounding Halton could be easily identified from existing aerial maps. One morning more than a thousand apprentices of Nos 1 and 2 Wings were ordered to parade on the grass-covered terrain adjacent to the Camp cinema. After forming up in some 30 or 40 lines, each apprentice stood to attention two yards distant from his immediate neighbour. In this way the whole area was covered with regular lines of apprentices.

It was intended that the resultant aerial view would be interpreted by the enemy as a plantation of young trees. We remained at the 'attention' for about ten minutes while an Avro *Tutor* slowly circled overhead taking aerial photographs. It would be interesting to know whether German pilots one day queried the young apple trees.

At about this time it was decided that the flat acre of land at the top of Bulbeck Hill behind No 1 Wing might be made suitable for an emergency airfield – or was it to prevent landings by enemy aircraft ? On sports afternoons during several weeks the whole of the station cleared away the countless loose stones from the ground. Without shovels or tools of any kind, the work became a game of moving larger stones from one small pile to another.

Stone-picking in fact was not a new pastime. Even in the early 'twenties the 250 boys of A Squadron No 1 Section (then the name for a Wing) had been paraded on the sports field in gymn kit armed with jack-knives and buckets. There on hands and knees they heard Sergeant Major 2 'Woof-Woof' Hayes say 'You are now ordered automatically forthwith to pick up every stone on the track'. Overseeing all this activity stood the youthful Flg Off W J Seward (who retired as AVM) together with the AOC, AVM Sir Charles Lambe. Every Saturday morning, the apprentices in each Section were allotted an area and when this had been cleared they could return to camp. It was thanks to Lambe and his stone-pickers that the present-day playing fields exist.[17]

My diary entry for 25 April 1938 reads 'in afternoon we went to Chalet and kicked stones into heaps'. The top of Bulbeck Hill behind No 1 Wing was known as the Chalet probably because of its six acres of attached land. Built in 1887 by Alfred de Rothschild and modelled on Queen Victoria's Swiss Cottage at Osborne in the Isle of Wight for his house guests, the hall – like Halton House still in use as the Officers' Mess – was emblazoned with the de Rothschild arms. Apprentices of pre-war vintage may not be aware that distinguished residents at the Chalet included Edward VIII when Prince of Wales, and even Winston

Churchill, who might well have witnessed their 'stone-picking' efforts.[18]

By 16 May, after it had become clear to even the dimmest that the work would never come to an end, I recorded 'stone picking seems to have finished'.

Meanwhile on a dark summer night in 1938 as a last farewell to Halton, the 32nd Entry selected for their attention an enormous four-wheel German naval gun which for many years had dominated Henderson Parade Ground. Perhaps to mark the deteriorating Anglo-German relations, numerous apprentices under cover of darkness using restraining ropes carefully lowered the two-ton monster from its traditional position behind the RAF pennant down the steep grass slope to a new firing position immediately overlooking the rear windows of No 1 Wing Headquarters.

At the passing out of the 33rd Entry in December 1938, Bill Sykes, then a Sergeant Apprentice, should have been the commander of the parade on No 4 Wing square. But this was one of the rare occasions when the ceremony had to be cancelled due to eight inches of snow on the square. He did in fact attend a Passing-Out Parade at Halton but only 35 years later, and then as Reviewing Officer with the rank of Air Vice-Marshal.[19]

At this juncture, in addition to the four Apprentices' Wings and No 5 (Airmens')Wing, the following units were stationed at RAF Halton: Princess Mary's Hospital; Medical Training Depôt; Institute of Pathology and Tropical Medecine; School of Cookery; Headquarters No 24(T) Group; No 9 Personnel Transit Centre; Nos 1 and 2 Medical Receiving Stations.[20]

Visit of H.M. King George VI

On 15 April 1939, *The Times* reported at length the visit to Halton of King George VI who was received by ACM Sir Cyril Newall and the AOC Halton, Air Cdre G. B. Dacre. The RAF, it said, claimed Halton with its 3,600 boys, including a number of naval air apprentices newly transferred from the RAF, to be the largest school in the world. Of those apprentices that had gone on to Cranwell cadetships, 65 had already reached the rank of squadron leader and 7 had commanded squadrons

Commenting on the day's menu, again according to *The Times*, the apprentices lunched that day on roast beef, baked potatoes, boiled carrots, followed by plum and apple tart with custard sauce – a meal fit for a King! At 'gunfire' (6.30 am), early morning tea and biscuits were served prior to physical training. Breakfast consisted of cornflakes, bacon and beef croquettes, tomato sauce and marmalade. For tea on the great day, there was roast ox-head with sage and onion, and for supper [surely an exceptional effort] steak and kidney pie and a milk drink. The misinformed reporter added that each apprentice received a pint of milk a day.

The next day, the King – who as a former flight commander in the Boys' Wing Cranwell knew something about training schools – sent a telegram to Halton saying he had greatly enjoyed his visit, and that he had been entirely satisfied with everything he had seen. In his reply, Air Cdre Dacre said, 'With humble duty I beg leave to thank Your Majesty for your encouraging message to all concerned with your visit to Halton which has been so greatly appreciated by all ranks'.[21]

Escorted by the AOC, HM George VI visits the Halton aerodrome on 14 April 1939.
(The Halton Magazine, Summer 1939.)

RAF Halton (Naval Wing) 1938-1942

Since the first world war, qualified RAF airmen volunteers had served in the Fleet Air Arm on aircraft carriers or at shore bases. In 1937 it was agreed that the Admiralty should provide the full manpower requirements of the FAA which would become effective in May 1939.

The first fifty directly enlisted FAA aircraft apprentices, selected after passing the entrance examination similar to that for RN artificers (introduced in 1904), began training on airframes or engines at No 4 Wing Halton in September 1938. Volunteers from RAF apprentices were called for – I hesitated but decided to stay on dry land – and several members of my entry transferred to the FAA as Naval Aircraft Apprentices while completing their training at Halton.

The transfers were made in January and June 1939 when a total of 169 apprentices made up from the 35th (82), 36th (64) and 37th (23) entries changed their light blue for naval uniforms.

By 2 September 1939, including their own direct entries, 459 naval apprentices were under training in No 4 Wing under naval administrative staff.

At this point they moved over to No 1 Wing to form under the command of Captain P H McCartan RN what was officially known as 'The Naval Wing', although RAF apprentices remained there to complete their training. Technical training at Halton was then speeded up by eliminating sports afternoons, drill sessions, and other non-essentials so as to compress the normal period of apprenticeship into two years without affecting the technical content of courses.

The naval 35th and 36th entries passed out together in December 1939, subsequent naval entries continued training at Halton up to the 42nd Entry, housed in No 1 Wing, which on its passing out on 29th July 1942, brought to an end the brief existence of RAF Halton (Naval) Wing.[22]

Halton declares war

During the summer of 1939 Halton was alive with rumours. On Saturday, 2nd September I wrote in my diary 'Confined to camp in afternoon, War looks imminent'. The next morning Neville Chamberlain made his nationwide broadcast when several hundred apprentices crowded round the radio in No 1 Wing canteen to hear the historic announcement. There was complete silence until the Prime Minister had finished. My diary entry reads 'listened to wireless at 11.15 a.m. War declared – chaps cheered!'

The outbreak of war affected our daily routine. The following Monday, we 'spent the day sandbagging the main entrance to the School'. Instead of sports on Wednesday afternoon, we 'cleared a wood for use by M.T. trucks'. On Thursday evening we had 'three small blue lights to see with'. By Friday I had recorded ' fatigues in evening – long hours are getting me down'. On 11th September we began a squadron servicing course and worked on Hawker *Hurricanes*. A week later the 35th Entry passed out from Halton at 6.30 a.m. before the trumpets had sounded reveille.

Routine became generally more monotonous with longer working days including Saturday afternoons. Relief was afforded by the fact that everyone knew that the war would accelerate the training programme and hasten the day to passing out. According to my five-year diary (I somehow managed to keep it going until 1942) by 7 September blackouts were the order of the day. In addition to drills wearing gas-masks, on 20 October I noted 'having to wear oilskins on backs and goggles on our glengarries – what a bind!' By then we were swotting for passing-out examinations and on 24 October – under a little blue light – I recorded 'did some General Studies in evening, weighed off Singapore'.

One week later we attended a lecture 'Why Germany went to war'. Armistice Day on 11th November 1939 was spent '. . . sandbagging all morning and just observed silence by knocking off at 11 a.m.'

The handwritten passing out results of the examinations held in mid-November – still carefully preserved at RAF Halton and available to personal callers only – show for the 36th Entry 10 LAC's and 242 AC1's of the 493 candidates in Nos 1 and 2 Wings. Although there were no cadetships awarded the above results show that Sgt App L R Old and Cpl App P D Richardson were recommended for Emergency Commissions.

On 30 November 1939 I noted, 'passing out dance – damn good. Sisters came over from RAF Hospital', this was unusual since it was probably the first occasion that females had been alowed to attend a Camp dance. The following morning, one day before my 18th birthday, I received my 'smoking pass' and thereby ceased to be an unauthorized smoker. But my newly won privilege was short-lived because before dawn on 13 December, the 36th Entry departed from Halton. In the total darkness of the parade ground it was difficult to find old friends to say goodbye. On leaving Wendover Station we went our different ways wondering when, if ever, we would meet again. My diary entry for that day happily reads '. . . finally passing out 4.30 a.m. – arrived 13 Maintenance Unit, Henlow at 10 o'clock'.

NOTES

6 Years of expansion (1937-1940)
1   Sdn Ldr P G Hering, *Customs and Traditions of the Royal Air Force,* 1961
2   *The Halton Magazine,*Summer 1932
3   *The Haltonian*, Winter 1985
4   *ibid*, Winter 1986; Hyde, op cit, pp 341, 353,418,427
    Report German Air Attaché to General Milch, 21.10.1937 (My translation: German Military Archives, Freiburg)
    The Aeroplane 27.10.1977
5   Andrew E Adam, *Beechwoods and Bayonets*, Buckingham, 1983
6   R H Kiernan, *Captain Albert Ball*, London 1933
    Debate on Air Estimates, *Hansard*, 31.3.1938
8   *The Haltonian,* Winter 1989 (Van 'Humpy' Gurr)
9   *ibid*, Winter 1987 (Bill Pugh)
10 *ibid*, Autumn 1983 (Harold Dewey: First Entry)
11 *ibid*, Summer 1989 (Matt Shead)
12 *ibid*, Summer 1992 (Dennis Adamson)
13 *ibid*, Summer 1991 (Charles Cave)
14 *ibid*, Winter 1990, Summer 1991
15 *ibid*, Winter 1991 (Alan Johnston)
16 *ibid*, Summer 1986, pp 10,38,39 (J Hughes/M E Cocker)
17 *ibid*, Winter 1988 (L W Clark 2nd Entry), *The Halton Magazine*, May 1954
18 *Daily Mail*, 19.6.1992 in *The Haltonian*, Winter 1992 (Frank Hitchcock)
19 *The Haltonian*, Summer 1986
20 Air 28/33

21 *The Halton Magazine,* Summer 1939
    NOTE
    King George V1 again visited RAF Halton on 23 July 1941, but all the
    aircraft apprentices had departed that same morning on summer leave.
    Senior officers present included AVM B E Sutton AOC No 24 Group, the
    AOC RAF   Halton, Air Cdre G B Dacre, Air Cdre J A Chamier,
    Commandant Air Trainng Corps and Mr J F Wolfenden, Director of Pre-
    Entry Training, Air Ministry. At No 2 Wing Headquarters he took the
    salute of a march past of cadets of the Air Training Corps. He then
    inspected the ATC Camp and cadets. Several such camps were being held
    for ATC boys in various parts of Britain. The camp at Halton provided for
    the 154 London-based Squadrons who could enjoy a week's holiday while
    seeing something of life at an Air Force training station. Some 500 boys a
    week passed through the camp during July to September. Subsequently the
    King inspected the training facilities at the aerodrome and the New
    Workshop. The airmen under training included flight mechanics and Fitters
    II (airframe or engines) whose courses were either 17 weeks or 9 weeks,
    respectively. The King finally inspected the Station Control Room and the
    Station Defence Company. During lunch he was entertained by No 3 Wing
    Military Band, consisting of volunteer trainees, which played on the
    hockey pitch in front of the Officers' Mess. Extracted from briefing notes
    sent to King George VI (RA GV1 PS 04230/143).
22 *The Haltonian,* Winter 1990 (Lee O'Reilly)

Chapter Seven

HALTON GOES TO WAR (1940-1945)

At the outbreak of war, apart from No 5 (Airmens') Wing, the 4,000 apprentices were housed in four self-contained wings, each under its own commanding officer with separate administration including mess-rooms, libraries, and recreation rooms. The undersized station cinema could not seat all those requiring tickets and certain shows were reserved for administrative staff and families. The apprentices of all wings continued to share the schools and workshops facilities including the large heated swimming pool.

On 1 September 1939, General Mobilisation of the Royal Air Force was ordered and on 3 September Halton received an Air Ministry signal announcing that war had broken out with Germany. Three days later four air raid messages were received between 7 am and 9 am obliging all personnel to seek cover in the shelter trenches. It was then found that the air raid had not taken place in the vicinity of Halton. Under the heading of 'Enemy Action' at least one Luftwaffe attack on Halton was noted on 2 August 1940 when unexploded bombs for a while became a problem.[1]

On several counts the 40th Entry is of particular interest. Thanks to their booklet *The Fortieth Entry – What happened to them* published in 1989, we know it was the last pre-war entry, the first intake reporting on 22 August 1939 and the second a week later. It was also the first wartime entry, since the third intake reported two days after the declaration of war. The total of 1,384 apprentices made the 40th the largest-ever entry with the shortest-ever training period of only twenty months.

After attestation at Halton, initially, the engine-apprentices were sent to RAF Cosford where in the raw winter conditions of 1939 the wooden huts compared unfavorably with the centrally-heated barrack blocks of Halton. Fortunately, in August 1940 it was decided that all apprentices including the instrument makers from Cranwell – the first apprentices since the 'twenties to have trained at both these schools – should return to Halton. On leaving Halton on 26 May 1941, those who had not reached the age of 17 1/2 years found themselves on RAF stations doing a man's job but still on apprentice pay of seven shillings a week.

Nevertheless, despite their accelerated training, no less than twenty members had managed to pass out as LAC's. Old hands on operational units were staggered to find thenmselves working alongside boy LAC's, some not even 18 years old.

With the RAF School of Cookery now located at Halton, meals served from the field kitchens sometimes showed an improvement over normal fare. Following the repatriation of airmen from the bombed beaches of Dunkirk, airmen without kit tried to purchase missing items from the apprentices. At the time of the London Blitz some apprentices clad only in pyjamas stealthily made their way to the hills behind the Camp to witness the searchlights and flashes of explosions only 30 miles distant.

To counter possible enemy invasion, apprentices were issued with bicycles and armed with Lee-Enfields and bandoliers of ammunition. Regular Saturday evening dances were organized by the local community of Aston Clinton in the Village Hall. With the relocation of the female staff of a radio firm at the village there was no shortage of partners

As far back as 1927, Paragraph 72 of *Apprentice Standing Orders* had stipulated 'Dances may be held in the Dining Halls of Nos 1, 2 and 4 Wings for Aircraft Apprentices only. No females are allowed to attend Aircraft Apprentices' dances.' But now for the first time in Halton's history, apprentices danced to the rhythm of a live band with real girls instead of in the barrack-room with a gramophone and apprentice partners.

To overcome the 21.00h deadline for booking-in at the guardroom, apprentice-dancers removed their identifying hatbands and brass wheels. The 30-minute return to the Camp involved crossing the Wendover-Tring road then up through the woods before negotiating the 'Gestapo-patrolled' stretch of 'grassy no-man's-land' and home. It seems that the No 1 Wing loose-paling emergency exit installed by the 24th Entry, mentioned elsewhere, was not on their escape-route.[2]

By October 1939, it had been thought there would be an acute shortage of Group I tradesmen throughout the Royal Air Force particularly Fitter II's.[3] But in November 1941 there was a surplus of 52,000 groundcrew, of which about half were fitters; by the following March the surplus fitters totalled 42,000. In 1944 no less than 27,000 airmen were transferred to the other services. As Air Chief Marshal Armitage comments in his Royal Aeronautical Society lecture at Halton in 1990, this surplus groundstaff was the result of grossly inaccurate estimates of the number of aircraft expected to reach the front line. This factor probably explains the dearth of wartime promotions for ex-apprentices after 1943!

Meanwhile for boys under military age, the Royal Air Force continued to recruit Apprentices. Admission continued to be by either competitive examination or direct entry which called for a School Certificate with credits in mathematics and an approved science subject. *Air Ministry Pamphlet No 15* set out in paragraph 3) the period of apprenticeship now only two years, and in paragraph 4) that attestation was 'for a period covering his apprenticeship and twelve years' regular service from the age of 18, that is, from the date of joining until he reaches the age of 30.' [4]

The WAAF at Halton

During 1941 the only intake of apprentices at Halton was the 43rd Entry in August with 185 boys. The scene at Halton the following spring was described by one WAAF, who arrived at Wendover Station on posting from the training centre at Gloucester. They had eaten their 'unexpired portion of the day's ration' consisting of fish-paste sandwiches packed tightly with a slice of cake, without paper, in a cloth bag. In the absence of transport and loaded down with steel-helmets and gas-masks, they began the two-mile trudge to the Camp dragging their kit-bags behind them. Fortunately they were noticed by several patients from the RAF Hospital who, in the customary bright blue 'pyjama-jacket' tunics, white shirts and red-ties, were identified by the girls as being RAF solely by their caps. The remainder of the journey was made in a hospital van.[5]

For a time after arrival at Halton they lived in wooden huts 'said to have been condemned for use by airmen'. After several months of typing personal occurrence reports (P.O.R.s), daily routine orders (D.R.O.s) and travel warrants, she acted as secretary to a flight-sergeant who moved, spoke and dictated on the run – undoubtedly an ex-Ruislip apprentice clerk ! The WAAF's, who wore navy-blue issue overalls over their uniforms, always carried gasmasks. During the monthly gas-alerts in addition to gasmasks on their chests, all ranks carried rolled gas-capes complete with 'quick-release' cords dangling from their shoulders.

In addition to leave, WAAFs were entitled to one S.O.P. (Sleeping-Out Pass) a month. Like the apprentices, the infrequent buses to Aylesbury meant that WAAF's seldom left Camp. By this time, weekly dances were held on the Camp – perhaps supplementing the traditional Aston Clinton 'hops'. Favourite numbers were the 'Paul Jones' and tangos played by the Station dance band whose signature tune was 'Dear one, the world is waiting for the sunrise'. Recent films were shown at the Camp Cinema and outside speakers included Franoise Rosay and – the now notorious – Tom Driberg.

The WAAF buildings were distinguished by a white 'passion-line' painted about ten feet distant from the walls. On returning to their billets in the evenings escorts were not allowed to pass this boundary – a rigorously enforced regulation which, presumably applying also to apprentices, effectively ruled out any lingering in the shadows ! Their once weekly 'camp night' – also enjoyed of course by the apprentices – was devoted to polishing the wood-block floors and washing and mending their smalls. Some of them consoled themselves by singing, to the tune of the tango *Jealousy*, what I have dubbed *The WAAF Refrain:*

'Twas all over my S.O.P.,
My crime was my wild S.O.P.;
For he was an officer in the RAF
And I was a poor little inn'cent WAAF.
He gave all his passion to me
And now I'm a mother-to-be.
I daren't tell my mother
That he was my lover . . .
'Twas all over my S.O.P.'

Polish apprentices at Halton

In March 1943 it was decided that 200 Polish Apprentices would form a separate Polish Squadron in No 1 Wing and a barrack block was taken over from No 2 Wing. Technical instruction was given in Polish by Polish officers and NCO's. The AOC Halton wrote to No 1 Wing commander listing the essential points in their training that had now been restored to peacetime standards.[6]

These Poles wore the usual apprentice-wheel on the left arm but incorporating the Polish Eagle at its centre. After training they were posted to Polish operational units. The unit known as No 2 (Polish) Air Apprentices School continued to train several entries of Polish Apprentices until its closure in November 1946.[7]

One evening a concert pianist, Solomon, played to a mixed Air Force audience which included a number of Polish apprentices. During his performance the pianist played a Polonaise from Chopin following which the Poles went beserk, cheering, clapping and even weeping . . . the RAF members of the audience had never witnessed such an emotional scene !

RAF Halton was represented at the Battle of Britain parade held in Aylesbury on 26 September 1943. At this time, 776 apprentices and 263 Polish apprentices were under training. The latter were inspected by the President of the Polish Republic, M Raczkiewicz accompanied by the Polish Commander-in-Chief on 17 December. Christmas was celebrated by training being suspended for three days.[8]

Reintroduction of three-years' training

The arrival at Halton in August 1943 of No 47 Entry, marked the reintroduction of the usual three-year period of training. Here we pick up the story from John Careless, author of *Trenchard's Brat*, and a member of this entry. At this time the No 1 Wing 'drums' of about 50 musicians still included sidedrums and, surprisingly, cymbals. The layouts of their steel-lockers continued to attract the interest of disciplinary NCO's. On the same shelf as their greatcoat and best-blue was a tin of dubbin with burnished lid together with the customary boot-polish and scrubbed brushes. The latter had apparently been promoted from their traditional position on the lower shelf of the wooden bedside-locker. Always on display were a pair of boots, rubber-knee (Wellingtons); boots with studded soles; and gym-shoes, all of which had to be polished including the rubber, soles, and even the studs. Over the two wall-pegs hung their webbing equipment but also steel helmet, gas mask and cape.

They had barely settled in when their room was 'ritually' raided by the senior, 44th Entry, wearing either woollen cap-comforters or school-caps whose upturned peaks were marked '44'. The scrambled beds and kit-lockers resulting from this raid, the first of many, had to be tidied up before lights-out at 21.45 h. Since only the senior entry was allowed out during the week, and with compulsory sports on Saturday afternoons and church parades on Sunday mornings, apprentices had little opportunity to venture outside the Camp.

Aircraft in the workshops included one *Spitfire,* a *Manchester* and two *Hampden* bombers, Hawker *Demons*, Miles *Magisters, Gipsy Moths* and *Tiger Moths*. Their first task in the basic metalwork course included the usual filing of a steel block now reduced in dimensions to 5 x 2 x ¼ inches. The hammer and chisel chipping of pre-war years had apparently been discontinued. The remainder of the technical training did not differ from that of pre-war days.

Jankers had become a more restrictive form of punishment for minor crimes. Offenders now wearing a white armband had to move all their kit into a wooden hut known as 'Croft's Cottage', so named after the corporal in charge. Another innovation for the 'wallahs' was a nightly kit layout following a parade at 20.00 h in best-blue and then a final turnout at 21.00 h in working dress. Another form of punishment were the 'check-parades' handed out by officers or nco's on the spot, and taking immediate effect, for one or more days. These involved hourly parades outside working hours, with alternately best-blue and working dress, until lights-out.

At the end of 1944, it was decided to move the Apprentices' Wing to RAF Cosford. Over a period of five days and evenings all the instructional material in the workshops and schools including mock-ups, aircraft components, books, etc, were loaded into railway trucks. Preceded by the senior entry, the remaining apprentices moved by special train to Cosford. The wooden huts, prefabricated school buildings, and fewer sports fields were a complete change from Halton. Only a week after their arrival the usual training had been resumed. One bonus was the regular outings to nearby Wolverhampton.

But after only ten weeks at Cosford they went through the full routine of returning to Halton. On arriving at Wendover, headed by the drums and pipes they marched back to Halton Camp to the rousing cheers of all the locals who surprisingly had turned out to welcome them. Back at the Camp they found that barbed wire now encircled the Apprentice Wing, laid down by Italian prisoners of war who had moved into the empty barracks of No 2 Wing. By this time, the strength at Halton amounted to about 11,000 personnel made up of 8,893 RAF and 1,975 WAAF.[9]

On Christmas Day 1944, the station dance band led by Sgt Carter was invited to play at Windsor Castle at a dance given by the Royal Household Staff. Those present included the King and Queen and the two princesses. A 'royal' letter of appreciation was later received by Sgt Carter.[10]

Halton celebrates victory in Europe

News of victory in Europe reached Halton on the evening of 7 May 1945 but only after 'bull night' preparations had been completed. According to one story, two signals had been transmitted the one being a general announcement of peace to all commands and the other a special explanation to RAF Halton which never knew the war had been on. In fact, the official account in the Operations Record Book for Halton reads 'The Camp received the news quietly and there was no undue celebrating'! [11]

Nevertheless, a crowd of jubilant apprentices on the square that night were soon joined by airmen and the WAAF's, normally never seen in that area. The celebrations, including an enthusiastic rendering by the pipes of *Black Bear*, went on until lights-out. Following the usual parade the next morning, the remainder of the day was proclaimed a holiday when many apprentices took off to enjoy the fun and games in London – a photograph reproduced in *The Haltonian* shows two members of the 47th Entry, distinguished by their three 'G.C.badges', in joyful mood seated on the bonnet of a grossly overloaded truck. At Halton the black paint was soon scraped from windows and full lighting restored while numbers of instructors donned civilian clothes instead of their uniform.

For V J Day, celebrated on 15 August, Jim Hughes (49th Entry) recalls that 'having been caught unprepared for VE Day, we thought that VJ Day would be better organized. It was, the Japanese surrendered while we were on summer leave'. [12]

Barely two weeks after the cessation of hostilities in Europe, and for Halton's Jubilee on 25 May 1945, two Marshals of the Royal Air Force were present. Lord Trenchard again as inspecting officer accompanied by the Chief of Air Staff, Sir Charles Portal, and other members of the Air Staff reviewed the 1,000 apprentices on parade commanded by Sgt Apprentice Meadows 'a veritable reincarnation of military smartness'. The five regular entries and the Polish apprentices, headed by the Apprentices' mascot, a goat dubbed Sgt Lewis, were accompanied by three bands all composed of apprentices including a drum-major who 'could do all the accepted juggling tricks with his staff'. The Polish band included silver trumpets having suspended red banners embroidered with the Polish eagle. Before taking the salute, Trenchard walked round the ranks of each squadron on parade. Particularly remarked upon were the straight, steady lines during the marchpast which drew rounds of applause from the spectators as was the fact that 'every apprentice as he stepped out looked the proudest young man in all Great Britain'.[13]

The 54-piece apprentice military band, of whom only four members knew anything about music before going to Halton, played that evening at the Officers Mess where Trenchard was guest of honour. During the dinner the Pipe Major played the *Wee MacGregor* while patrolling the tables. Afterwards Trenchard was presented with a framed roll of honour giving the names of all those apprentices who had been decorated or commissioned. In his response, Trenchard said, 'we celebrate not only the Jubilee but the part Halton played in smashing Germany'. Portal in a tribute to Trenchard said, 'He has led the Air Force through its days of difficulty sometimes almost of disaster. He has seen the result of the work you do here displayed by your predecessors'. Of the 18,499 apprentices that had passed through Halton up to May 1945, 4,143 had been commissioned.[14]

In Trenchard's speech reported in the Christmas 1945 edition of *The Halton Magazine*, he said that Churchill's famous 'Never have so many owed so much to so few' applied almost more to them than any others who had been in the Royal Air Force. They had been the means by which the spearhead in defence of the Empire had worked . . .

NOTES

7   Halton goes to war (1940-1945)

1   Air 28/33
2   *The Haltonian*, Summer 1992 (Jack Neville)
3   Air 20/1347, Note on history of RAF training, A.M.Jan 1945, p 237
4   *ABC of the RAF*, 1941, pp 10,11
5   Imp War Mus, Mrs N C Walton 88/2/1
6   Air 20/1371
7   *The Haltonian*, Summer 1984 (Mr Wilson)
8   Air 28/33
9   RAF Halton at War 1939-45: A 'Miscellany'
10   Air 28/33
11   Air 28/33 (8.5.1945); Adam, op cit, p 111
12   *The Haltonian*, Winter 1985 (Jim Hughes); Air 28/33
13   *Flight,* 31.5.1945; Armitage, op cit
14   Air 28/337

Chapter Eight

POST-WAR HALTON (1945-1993)

For the first time since the war, Guy Fawkes night 1945 was celebrated throughout Britain. Although this freedom did not extend to RAF Halton the apprentices in No 1 Wing decided otherwise. John Careless (47th Entry) in his book *Trenchard's Brat* described the celebrations at Halton. A mockup tank consisting of piled up railway sleepers had been built by RAF Regiment instructors for their assault course on the grassy slope behind No 1 Apprentice Wing. Just before nightfall barrels of creosote, stacked conveniently near for reroofing huts of the School of Cookery, were poured over the pile.

With hissing fireworks and coloured Verey lights, the latter by courtesy of the armourers, the flaming beacon became the centrepiece for jubilant apprentices urged on by the skirl of the bagpipes. The fire brigade arrived accompanied by Service Policemen, the Orderly Officer as well as airmen from No 2 Wing. Meanwhile, the fire-hose failed to reach the conflagration because apprentices at the pump-end succeeded in dragging the hose, plus struggling fire-crew, back down the hill. When the unequal tug-of-war finally ended the fire had lost its fury. The crew climbed on the tender ready to drive off but could not start the engine because someone had apparently removed the sparking plugs. Apart from a twopenny barrack-damages charge levied against each member of No 1 Wing, nothing more was heard about the incident.

Barrack-room barbers still practised their illegal craft, while another source of revenue for hardup apprentices was selling unused cigarette and sweet coupons. Motorcycles were still not allowed, and in any case petrol was rationed, but with anti-gas eyeshields serving as goggles several apprentices, who kept their machines in local garages, became acquainted with the hills and dales of Buckinghamshire.

A large proportion of the apprentices in the 47th Entry – the first post-war entry to complete the normal three-year course, and the first to be trained on jet engines – had been accepted for aircrew training, while from the thirty recommended for commissions two technical and two flying cadetships were awarded. They marched off after the passing out parade between the ranks of junior entries with the pipes playing Auld land Syne.[1]

One corporal MT driver on return from overseas at the end of 1945, who spent his last months of service at Halton, disrespectfully referred to it as 'this monument to the Great Lord of Bull'. Apart from the large transport section and the Apprentices' School, other units at Halton then included the School of Tropical Medicine, the Queen Mary RAF Hospital, the School of Cookery, vast stores' sheds and the large well-equipped workshops. During the weekly barrack-room inspections, the Commanding Officer was accompanied by the Orderly Officer, usually a warrant officer whose white-gloved hands swept the tops of lockers searching for dust.

The Salvation Army Canteen, or 'Sally Anne' as it was known, was not only warm but sold better tea and 'wads' than did the NAAFI. Although Halton was then the home of the School of Cookery the quality of the food at least in the Airmens' Mess was poor, even with allowance for the rationing still in force. Numerous platefuls of food were tipped directly into the overflowing swill-bins. In spite of all this, the corporal insisted that if he had to choose again which uniform to wear he would still opt for Air Force blue and the 'old firm'.[2]

RAF Halton Glider Flight

In March 1945 the RAF Halton Glider Flight, first mooted by the AOC-in-C Technical Training Command the previous year, was set up and the first batch of 21 Apprentices selected from third-year students began their training up to solo standard. Volunteers from Station permanent staff assisted with the organization of the gliding which took place after working hours on a recreational basis.

To begin with two ancient Mk I Kirby *Cadets* were employed, soon to be replaced by Mk II's. When in 1949 a two-seater Kranich was acquired exceptional pupils could extend their training to circuit flying. Well over five thousand launches were made that year and from 388 pupils given instruction 47 reached solo standard. In 1950 Slingsby Sedbergh *T21* trainers with side-by-side seats replaced the older machines.

Meanwhile until it was disestablished in 1974, the *Ansons* and *Tiger Moths* in the Station Flight continued to give apprentices their air experience. With the smaller entries of apprentices, qualified glider instructors could no longer be found from Apprentice flight commanders. In 1985 the winch-launched gliders were replaced by the *Venture* motor-glider which enabled each apprentice to make a 20-minute flight with hands-on experience. By 1987 two Education Officers, one Medical (Sec) Officer and one Sergeant (A Tech E) were qualified to give instruction. Those showing enthusiasm were encouraged to join either the Gliding Club or the Flying Club both located on the Station. Apprentices were thus encouraged to take an interest in flying from the outset of their training. This not only assisted them in their technical studies but was the first step towards flying training which traditionally they could apply for towards the end of their Halton training. This opportunity had always existed from the inception of Trenchard's Apprenticeship scheme.[3]

Reverting to the immediate post-war period, in October 1945 it was announced that the apprentice scheme would be expanded with three intakes of 500 apprentices each year. But the response averaged only 150 per entry, fortunately with the continuation of National Service qualified recruits could be trained for technical posts. The threat posed by the Soviet Union and the Korean War in 1950 led to a full-scale rearmament programme but despite this entries remained comparatively small.

Apprentice scheme expanded

By 1946 English and General Studies came under a Head of Department, Sdn Ldr F W Clarke who had been posted back to Halton, while intermediate examinations in all school subjects had now been re-established. As in pre-war days, the aim of the General Studies course was to give apprentices a broader and deeper understanding of the kind of problems facing them during their service in all parts of the globe. But not all apprentices were enthusiastic about the educational prospects now opening up. The following piece taken from the summer number of the Halton Magazine signed 'Noddah' expressed one apprentice's resignment to the educational climate:

THE PICTURE ON THE WALL

When of theory I am weary, and the lesson seems too long,
And the Education Officer goes droning, droning on;
If he does not ask us questions and is not wont to call,
I recede into the glamour of the picture on the wall.
I have lost my third dimension while I wander where I will,
Through the pine woods by the river, to the castle on the hill
Where I watch the great ships sailing at a changeless, timeless rate,
Which is just the rate one moves at in a two-dimension state.
In this world of changeless seasons, and of endless summer day
My spirit roams at random o'er the hills beside the bay,
Till my silent dream is shattered when to break I have to run,
For the state of two dimensions will not do for milk and bun.

At this time the entrance examination to Halton was modified to include an intelligence test and special aptitude testing. The winter of 1946/7 placed a severe strain on most Air Force stations and with fuel shortages Halton closed down for a short period. In March 1947 a Soviet delegation headed by M Fadeev, General Secretary of the Union of Soviet Writers, visited Halton. The following month at a flying demonstration by aircraft of the Royal Air Force, the principal guest was General Piollet, Chief of Staff, French Air Force accompanied by Mr Atlee, Prime Minister and the Chief of the Air Staff.[4]

Then for the next comparatively settled ten years up to 1964 Halton assumed an international character with apprentices hailing from as far afield as Rhodesia, Ceylon, Pakistan, Brazil and Venezuela.

From 1961 onwards the number of apprentices per entry dropped to less than 500 a year, and again from 1966 to below 100, until by 1973 the 122nd Entry consisted of only 20 entrants. At that point someone had a change of mind because for the two-year period 1974/5 the figure increased to 824 apprentices. But by the following year the 127th Entry had fallen again to 98 apprentices.

To revert to the general training of apprentices at Halton, the Rt Hon Arthur Henderson in addressing the 60th Entry on their passing out in 1951 reminded those on parade that 75% of the officers now serving in the Royal Air Force had served in the ranks. On the same occasion, MRAF Sir John Slessor, also attending the parade, said that all had a very fair chance of reaching commissioned rank.[5]

The reviewing officer at the passing-out parade of the 62nd Entry the following May was Marshal of the Royal Air Force Lord Tedder. 'There is no parade', reported *the Flight* representative present 'quite like a Halton passing-out.

HM Queen Elizabeth, with the AOC Air Cdre J G W Weston behind the piled drums, presenting her Colour to No 1 School of Technical Training. The shot featuring Sgt App Colour Bearer F M A Hindes, who retired as Wing Commander, appeared for several years in the opening to British Movietone News.

(Courtesy of *Bucks Advertiser.*)

But of a total of 126 boys no fewer than 66 had left the Entry through discharge, sickness, transfer to other schools or recoursing to later intakes. Commenting on In precision it is equal to the best the professional soldiers can show, and yet it is entirely in the hands of the apprentices – none of the staff is on parade'. this in his address, after distributing the prizes, Lord Tedder referred to those passing out as 'survivors' which was a good thing because the Royal Air Force had to maintain its high standard. In stressing the importance of teamwork he said that in NATO it was the airmen who were setting the pace for teamwork.[6]

To mark the presentation of the Queen's Colour that year, a special 100-page edition of *The Halton Magazine* was published (see Appendix B). It was recorded that during the ceremony Her Majesty displayed a lively interest in all she saw and particularly in the Halton goat mascot who, overcome by the heat and probably the occasion, fell fast asleep in the shade cast by the legs of his apprentice keeper.[7]

Changes in training methods

At the passing out parade of the 64th Entry in December 1952, Air Cdre J G W Weston reported that changes in equipment had been made to enable apprentices to be taught the theory and practice necessary for them to perform their duty in a modern air force. The syllabus was being revised so as to place more emphasis on the teaching of fundamental knowledge and less on details.[8]

On 27 March 1953, Lord de L'Isle and Dudley, Secretary of State for Air, reviewed the Passing Out Parade of the 65th Entry. He emphasized that the apprentices would have many ups and downs in their careers – hopefully more ups than downs. He reminded them that despite the progress in science nothing could replace the qualities of leadership, study and forceful example which were just as necessary on the ground as in the air. He had no doubt they would take advantage of the great opportunities that lay ahead to prove themselves.[9]

On 2 June, 45 apprentices accompanied by the Halton Apprentices Military Band took part in the Coronation Parade forming part of the Royal Air Force contingent lining Regent Street. During the summer all technical instructional staff were grouped under a Technical Training Wing in order to facilitate control and co-ordination of instruction. A further innovation introduced 'advanced' and 'normal' courses in educational training for the 71st and subsequent entries.

In October, Air Marshal Sir Francis J Fogarty reminded those graduating that Halton Apprentices were the backbone of the Royal Air Force. Their outstanding predecessors at the great school during the piston-age had included that illustrious ex-apprentice Air Cdre Sir Frank Whittle (see App G). Now it was their turn to take up the challenge and to provide the backbone for the jet and guided missile age of the future.[10]

The celebration of Guy Fawke's Night had now become something of a tradition at Halton with the armourers enjoying their annual fling at amusing all the children – and others. It fell to Air Cdre J G W Weston CB OBE to fire the customary first mortar of the evening, while Mrs Weston did her part by igniting a monster bonfire.

Also in 1953, Gp Capt E Knowles MBE, who had taught Halton apprentices back in the early days, was appointed Principal Education Officer. The editor of *The Halton Magazine* commented that he was well acquainted with some of the more ingenious ways the apprentices had of expressing their personalities. Beginning with the 70th Entry, success in the Progress Examinations was to count for the award of the National Certificate. In this connection, Cpl App Benson was among the fifteen, out of 5,500 in Britain who had obtained National Certificates that year, to be awarded a Whitworth Prize. It was decided that the School Library would henceforth be known as The Trenchard Library, which housed Trenchard's private collection of books.[11]

An Airfield Training Squadron was set up under the administration of the Technical Training Wing. The Halton Society which had flourished almost from the inception of the apprentice scheme, now included 25 sections such as film-making and even campanology and provided assistance for apprentices participating in the pursuits section of the Duke of Edinburgh's Award Scheme.[12]

Lord Trenchard's last parade at Halton

In August 1955 Trenchard, for the last time, reviewed the passing out of the 175 members of the 57th Entry. A report in *The Aeroplane* praised the apprentices drill during the parade – particularly their slow march, notorious difficult to achieve – accompanied by the music of three apprentice bands. Meanwhile the commandant Air Cdre Rutter mentioned the improved technical standards achieved and the many visits made to the factories of aircraft, engine and component manufacturers. Of those graduating no less than 70% had volunteered for aircrew training while eleven apprentices had gained gliding certificates.

In his address, Trenchard explained that originally Halton had been planned for 3,000 apprentices but had been enlarged to take 4,000 with plans for another school. He only regretted that there were now so few apprentices compared with what he had envisaged thirty years before. He hoped that by their keeness and pride others might recognize the value of their training. They should work hard so as to derive the maximum benefit from their training. The apprentices who were the hope of the world should let them know that the Air Force was efficient and that its aircraft would be kept in the air.

As in the Battle of Britain, they might have to make one aircraft do the work of two because they were always short of aircraft at the beginning. He defined discipline as playing the game with seniors, equals and juniors. He wished them luck and hoped that by their example and influence Halton would be built up again to its former size. After visiting the various sections at Halton, including workshops, he accepted to become President of the Halton Branch of the Royal Aeronautical Society.[13]

Since the earliest days relations between Aylesbury and Halton Camp had always been close. This link was formalized when on 24 April 1956, the Borough of Aylesbury conferred upon the 'Officer Commanding and all ranks of the Royal Air Force Station, Halton for the time being and from time to time stationed at Halton the privilege, honour and distinction henceforth and for ever of marching through the streets of Aylesbury upon all ceremonial occasions with bayonets fixed, colours flying, drums beating and bands playing'. The Commandant, Air Cdre Tindall-Carill-Worsley, signed the parchment roll on behalf of the Station in his newly conferred status as a Freeman of the Borough.

BOROUGH OF AYLESBURY.

ROLL OF HONORARY FREEMEN.

NUMBER	
NAME AND DESCRIPTION OF FREEMEN.	The Officer Commanding and All Ranks of The Royal Air Force Station, Halton.
DATE OF MEETING OF THE COUNCIL WHEN RESOLUTION WAS PASSED CONFERRING THE HONORARY FREEDOM OF ENTRY INTO THE BOROUGH.	DATE OF PRESENTATION OF CERTIFICATE AND SIGNING OF THE ROLL.
Monday, the 13th February, 1956.	Tuesday, the 24th April, 1956.

RESOLUTION.

That in recognition of the most friendly association which has always existed between the Borough Council, the People of Aylesbury and the Men and Women of the Royal Air Force stationed at Halton the Council do confer upon the Officer Commanding and all ranks of the Royal Air Force for the time being and from time to time stationed at Halton the privilege, honour and distinction henceforth and for ever of marching through the streets of Aylesbury upon all ceremonial occasions with bayonets fixed, colours flying, drums beating and bands playing.

SIGNATURE OF FREEMAN.   G. T. Carill-Worsley
                                            Air Commodore.

FOR AND ON BEHALF OF THE
ROYAL AIR FORCE STATION, HALTON.

WITNESSES.

William T. Brookes
                    MAYOR.

                    TOWN CLERK.

Apprentices of the 80th Entry passing out in April 1958 were no doubt surprized when Air Marshal Sir Gilbert Nicholette KBE CB AFC – who had just retired from the Royal Air Force – after expressing the hope that those leaving Halton would all enjoy long and successful careers added, 'I wish that I were in your shoes'.[14]

Between 1959 and 1963 a limited number of Dental Technician Apprentices were trained at Halton who graduated with the Intermediate and Final Certificates of Dental Technology of the City and Guilds of London. An unusual feature of the passing out of the 84th Entry in July 1959 was the presence of a Warrant Officer Apprentice J Gilbert who commanded the parade.[15]

The final results of the 88th Entry that passed out in December 1960 show that 4 apprentices were promoted Corporal and 10 to Corporal Technician after one year, with 75 for promotion after a period of two years and three months.[16]

During the first two terms of 1961, Wing Commander Kimber – author of the first history of Halton – returned to his former school as lecturer in applied mathematics. He found much had changed since his own time there thirty years before. He again revisited Halton in 1967, but this time as CO of the Combined Cadet Course at the Blue Coat School (Reading). While his contingent of cadets marched to the dining-hall for their lunch a group of NCO's commented on the smartness of the boys. Kimber was surprised when one Sergeant told him he would not see that sort of thing here. Nevertheless, only two years later as reviewing officer at the Graduation Parade of the 93rd Entry at Halton in 1963, Admiral of the Fleet, Earl Mountbatten of Burma, recalled that their troops including 20,000 Chindits had relied on the RAF both for supplies and air cover. The army had been on half-rations and the Air Force on double duty. He added that if the Battle of Waterloo had been won on the playing fields of Eton, equally it could be said that the Battle of Burma was won in the Training School at Halton.[17]

Adaptation of training methods

Training methods again had to be adapted from about 1964 to match sophisticated aircraft such as the ill-fated TSR2 whose complex design called for fault diagnosis in systems and component replacement by manufacturers. The 106th Entry, whose training ended in December 1966, was the last entry of aircraft apprentices under the original Lord Trenchard scheme. The new youth training scheme at Halton instituted in 1964 provided training for: a) Technician Apprentices (Entry numbers commenced at 107) who followed a three-year course and after a further two years' training at selected stations could become systems engineers and eventually diagnosticians; b) Craft Apprentices (Entry numbers commenced at 201 and ended at 231) who followed a two-year course.[18]

By the summer of 1966 Apprentices had evolved and as an article in *The Halton Magazine* put it, they now belonged to the 'with it' generation. The

Royal Air Force, the author wrote, not wanting to be regarded as 'square' or to become fair game for vicious reporters of certain daily newspapers had frequently updated the standing orders for Apprentices. The *Rules for Apprentices* (1936) were then compared with those proposed for the 1966 vintage Apprentice:

Apprentice Rules 1936	Proposed Apprentice Rules 1966
Snowballing within Station is forbidden.	Snowballing of officers above the rank of Group Captain is not encouraged.
Trading within the camp is forbidden.	Purple-heart salesmen are not permitted in the NAAFI.
Hair cutting by Boy Entrants is forbidden.	Hair must be neatly tied back with a ribbon.
Wireless sets in barrack rooms are forbidden.	Fruit machines are not to be used when BBC 2 is on.
No Boy Entrants may keep fire-arms.	Apprentices are to check their weapons in at the armoury before entering the camp.
Boy Entrants are forbidden to associate with females.	Apprentices are forbidden to have females in the barrack quarters from 0800 to 2000.
Bicycles are not be ridden on any pathways.	Cars are not to be kept in the barrack rooms.

Kermode Hall

Early in 1969 the decision was made to rename the school building as Kermode Hall to commemorate the name of the illustrious member of the Education Branch whose life had been dedicated to the RAF apprentice and cadet systems at Halton and Cranwell (a fuller account of his achievements is given in Appendix D). Air-Vice Marshal A C Kermode CBE, MA, FRAeS had retired from the Air Force as Director of Educational Services in 1960. Following service as a pilot in the RNAS and RAF in the first World War he went up to Cambridge where in 1921 he obtained an honours degree in the Mechanical Science Tripos. Two years later after flying as an observer at the Royal Aircraft Establishment he became a civilian education officer. Until 1939 he taught aeronautical engineering subjects to some 10,000 Aircraft Apprentices and Technical Officers at Halton, Cranwell and Henlow. The whole of his twelve years at Halton before leaving in 1936 was devoted to the welfare of the apprentices. The Editor of the *Halton Magazine* at that time wrote of him '. . . Kermode has qualified for a very special niche, not only by his length of residence but by the whole-hearted devotion he has given to the Halton Society, and all those other activities which have, as their object. the making of a fuller life for every Aircraft Apprentice' [19]

More changes in training
In 1969 a distinguished Army officer, General Sir Charles Harrington KCB DSO MC, reviewed the 110th Entry of Technical Apprentices and the 312th Entry of Administrative Appentices (one-year course). Coming from a 'Pongo' – as Army-types were disrespectfully dubbed by apprentices – his forthright remarks on this occasion included the following homily: '. . . . I am not going to say to those of you who didn't win a prize that you are equally as good as they are, and that your day will eventually come. Your day will come when you pull your fingers out! You only achieve anything by hard work and a bit of natural ability, and also of course a bit of luck'.[20]

The Queen escorted by the Station Commander, Gp Capt O J Truelove MBE, is welcomed with a bouquet of flowers.

(*The Haltonian*, Summer 1981.)

At the passing out of the 111th Entry in October 1969, the Commandant, Air Cdre R H G Weighill CBE DFC, revealed one or two behind-the-scene aspects of an AOC's daily routine at Halton, certainly hitherto unsuspected by apprentices:

> '. . . You would be surprised how well you get to know a bunch of chaps who march past your house four times a day, making sure they are not noticed employing as many as four bands to mark their progress – I can now tell you that the best vantage point in my house to watch from is, in fact, the upstairs lavatory. I am told that one distinguished Commandant so ordered his life that he could yell suitable encouragement from there each morning. I have not quite reached that stage yet although my small daughter gives a running commentary the whole time they are marching by!'[21]

The 70's and 80's saw important changes in training, from what had been essentially a military boarding school. There was now an enriched form of academic and engineering training for those graduating with the status of technicians. Apprentices of the small entries were now well-qualified academically before entering Halton and most could expect to obtain a formal engineering qualification on completion of their Halton training.[22]

Those present at a review in 1972 to celebrate 50 years of Halton included ACM Sir John Grandy, Chief of the Air Staff, and Air Marshal Sir Kenneth Porter, senior serving ex-apprentice, then AOC-in-C RAF Maintenance Command. Also present was Sdn Ldr A J Akehurst, the very first apprentice at Halton and also first Secretary of the Old Haltonians.[23]

A further change in training announced in October 1973 was implemented in the new year with the 123rd Entry whose members became Apprentice Engineering Technicians (A and P) – airframe and propulsion. On completion of their dual-skill training they passed out as Junior Technicians. Examination requirements for entry called for four GCE 'O' level subjects, or CSE grade 1, two of which had to be mathematics and physics or engineering science, or a similar alternative.[24]

By 1974, the distinctive coloured hat-bands, chevrons and even the apprentice wheel-badge had been abolished (only to be reintroduced in 1982). The Halton apprentice badge had been worn since 1918 when it had been intended to distinguish the men from the boys ! A letter 'B' had originally featured in the centre of the propellor boss, but for obvious reasons it had been omitted from the approved four-bladed propellor design.[25]

In 1983, Apprentice ranks which had played a major role in matters of discipline and leadership were being reintroduced, the term 'senior student' replacing 'leading aircraft apprentice'. Weekly pay rates varied according to age from £18.30 for those under 16½ years to £38 – at 17½. Annual leave entitlement by now had increased to nine weeks with fairly frequent weekend passes. As well as railway warrants, cash-allowances for petrol could be claimed by car owners. At least from 1975 onwards married apprentices became eligible for married quarters at Halton.[26]

Eagle Block – formerly 'Block 12' – and Author.
(Author's Photo.)

Meanwhile during 1978 the 130th Entry had moved into 'Anson Block' the first of the barrack-blocks to be converted into four-man rooms complete with fitted wardrobes and carpets. On each each floor a one-man room was set aside for the 'floor leader'. By 1988 launderettes and TV rooms were also available.[27]

Exactly 138 days before their graduation on 17 October 1984, the 138th Entry anticipated the completion of their training at Halton. High spots included: a bicycle 'flying' from the station flag-pole, a banner along station headquarters, the flight-sergeant's office moved completely to the stage in Kermode Hall, new parking-slot names for instructors. Despite all this, 91 apprentices of the original 106 to arrive at Halton obtained BTEC Higher Certificates, equivalent to the old Higher National Certificate, which academically qualified them for entry to a commission in the Engineer Branch.[28]

Compared with this, the passing out of the 139th Entry was uneventful except for a low-flying private aircraft towing the banner ' 139th Entry – the end of an era' which evoked spontaneous applause from the spectators at the parade.[29]

In his report on the 146th Entry in 1988, Gp Capt SMD Williamson-Noble confirmed that the dual-skilled, airframe and propulsion, Aircraft Engineering Apprentice at Halton fully met the governmental definition of a technician laid down in the 1969 *Haslegrave Government Committee Report*, that is one 'required to exercise judgement in the sense of both diagnosis and appraisal, and initiative in his work; is frequently called upon to supervise the work of others . . .'[30]

The 148th Entry's graduation on 25 October 1989 was honoured by the presence, as Reviewing Officer, of Air Marshal Sir Eric Dunn, KBE CB BEM CEng MRAeS, who had begun his career as an Aircraft Apprentice with the 48th Entry before retiring as Chief Engineer of the Royal Air Force. As the Station Commander's report put it, such an outstanding career left no doubt that a Halton Apprenticeship provided the best start for an Engineer. Of the 72 members of the 148th who arrived at Halton from the School of Recruit Training at Swinderby, 12 had immediately exercised their right to voluntary discharge, 4 were remustered to other trades and 2 were discharged from the RAF. A total of 26 apprentices obtained the Higher National Certificate.[31]

Au revoir Halton

The graduation of the 46 members of No 155 Entry which took place on 24 June 1993 with the Duke of Gloucester as Reviewing Officer, marked the end of Apprentice training at No 1 School of Technical Training RAF Halton. This occasion was suitably commemorated by a Royal Salute overflown by the *Red Arrows*, a *VC 10*, 4 *Harriers* and 5 *Hercules* whose crews included a number of serving ex-apprentices. Two support flights that day included a mix (seen only at RAF Halton parades) of serving ex-apprentices ranking from junior technician up to group captain commanded by Air Commodore Dick Bogg (91 Entry). The members of No 155 Entry formed the Escort Squadron for The Queen's Colour.

Awaiting the arrival of the Duke of Gloucester, Bill Kelley, Editor of *The Haltonian*, described the stillness disturbed only by the chattering of the swallows as they swooped overhead against the background of the beech trees shining in the sun, a setting which formed a perfect memory to take away from this place which held so many memories, both good and bad, for thousands of ex-Haltonians. The last command was given by Sergeant Apprentice, Engineering Technician Humphrey: 'The 155th and final entry of Halton Apprentices will march off'. The Halton hills echoed the final volley of blanks as the flight marched out of view.[32]

But it was not until the graduation on 7th October 1993 of the Avionics members of No 155 Entry at RAF Cosford (see Appendix H) that the RAF

Graduation parade of No 155, the last Apprentice Entry at RAF Halton, on 24 June 1993, with the Duke of Gloucester as Reviewing Officer.

(Via HAAA.)

No 155 Entry at RAF Cosford marching past ex-apprentice Air Marshal Sir Arthur Dunn following the command 'The last and final entry of Royal Air Force Apprentices will march off'.

(Author's Photo.)

Aircraft Apprentice Scheme finally ended. Shortly after my arrival at Cosford for the graduation ceremony I found myself walking up an otherwise deserted Camp road leading to the Parade Ground. There I fell in with Mr and Mrs Jones whose son, they told me proudly, would that morning be receiving the Royal Aeronautical Society Prize. Only a minute or two later the graduating flight passed us as they moved up towards the Square. Their impeccable turnout and marching could only have been equalled by the Brigade of Guards. I was reminded, however, that it was a Royal Air Force unit by the 'Morning John' greeting from Mr Jones immediately acknowledged from the ranks by a very happy 'Morning Dad'!

Their aerospace (avionics) and electronic engineering course to Higher National Certificate level – six months longer than the corresponding No 155 Halton entry – was described by Gp Capt M J Gilding, Station Commander, as '3½ years elective application of hardship'. He reflected with sadness the end of a proud tradition of apprentice training in the Royal Air Force. The reviewing officer, once again Air Marshal Sir Eric Dunn, expressed the hope that all these youngsters who had excelled in their engineering and military training would grasp the opportunities when they occurred on entering the Royal Air Force at such an exciting time.

Sgt App W Rudge with his three prizes at the Graduation of No 155 Entry – the final Apprentice Entry – RAF Cosford on 7 October 1993.

(Author's Photo.)

Again as at Halton, visitors were intrigued at the composition of No 2
Support Flight, consisting of serving ex-apprentices of all ranks, under Wg Cdr
A Renshaw RAF, commanding Technical Training Wing RAF Cosford. Many
of the audience smiled on hearing the unusual command 'Executives fall in'
when the wing commander and two senior aircraftmen took up posts as the three
flight commanders.

Once more Royal Air Force pilots overflew the parade with seven different
aircraft types including three *Victors* also making their last appearance on the
disbanding of No 55 Squadron, RAF Marham. Following the inspection, No 155
Entry led by the Parade Commander, Sergeant Apprentice Technician W Rudge,
proudly marched off the Parade Ground to the strains of Auld Land Syne played
by the Western Regional Band of the Royal Air Force. Their final 'West-Point'
hats-in-the-air act – contrary to good order and discipline, but heartily
applauded by those present including four previous station commanders –
concluded the heartwarming ceremony.

Now that the RAF Apprentice Scheme has ended, Gp Capt G O Burton (100
Entry), Commandant of RAF Halton, has emphasized the increasingly important
role of the Halton Aircraft Apprentices Association for future years as well as
the triennial reunions which serve to remind participants of their special
privilege of being an ex-apprentice.[32]

Something about Halton has for many years brought ex-apprentices back
in their thousands to these reunions. On the aerodrome there is always a
scratch performance by an 'oldies' pipe-band complete with volunteer
drummers and mace-bearer some clad in gorgeous tartans. An old favourite is
when the pipers play the banned Halton-version of *Black Bear* with its stirring
'Aye' responses in the right places. Old, and not so old, boys can be seen
walking, some shuffling, through the carpet of yellow leaves in Chestnut
Avenue leading to Kermode Hall and the Trenchard Library – where they might
have done their swotting. The day traditionally closes with the oldest Halton
entries leading the march-up past Main Point and that hill to Henderson Parade
Ground.

Sadly we shall no longer be able to watch the Apprentice Drill Squad
with their three hundred movements carried out in complete silence with
not even an 'educated' reminder to hold their heads up ! All ex-apprentices
admitted that this display outshone anything they ever did while senior
entries quietly reflected that even old Bonham would have conceded a grudging
'Yes'.

At the conclusion of my recent visit to RAF Halton it was almost dark when I
stood alone on Wendover Station awaiting the next up-train. What I still
remember, and this in the gathering dusk, was the white WAY OUT sign on the
footbridge. For those who wanted Halton it should read WAY IN . . . but as Air
Vice-Marshal Reid said in his Foreword to this book 'that's enough from an old
hand'.

Wendover Station – Au revoir Halton.

(Author's Photo.)

Colour Hand Over by ACM Sir Michael Armitage KCB CBE (56th) to Cosford Colour Officer.

In November 1994, to mark the transfer of No 1 School of of Technical Training from Halton to Cosford, the Queen's Colour was ceremoniously handed over. ACM Sir Michael Armitage was accompanied by the Halton Station Commander Gp Capt Geoffrey Burton, both ex-apprentices. Numerous ex-apprentices watched as the Queen's Colour, escorted by two flights of Halton personnel, was entrusted to the Cosford contingent who then marched off the Colour for the last time.

But tradition dies hard. Direct entrants to the Royal Air Force who in future complete their initial training at the station will still be able to say 'I too was at Halton'.

NOTES

8 Post-war Halton (1945-1993)

1 Careless, op cit, pp 26-37; *The Halton Magazine*, Summer 1946
2 Imp War Museum, L E Ransom 87/42/1
3 L Fellows, 'RAF Halton Glider Flight', *Air Clues*, June 1987, pp 231-4; *Halton Magazine*, Summer 1948, 'The Cold War and Halton'.
4 'Aircraft Apprentice Training at Halton' 1958 (HAAA)
5 *The Halton Magazine*, February 1952
6 *Flight*, 6.6.1952
7 *The Halton Magazine*, September 1952
8 *Flight*, 26.12. 1952
9 *The Halton Magazine*, May 1953
10 *ibid*, October 1953
11 *ibid*, Feb 1954
12 'Aircraft Apprentice Training at Halton' 1958 (HAAA)
13 *The Aeroplane*, 18.8.1955
14 *The Halton Magazine*, Summer 1953
15 *The Haltonian*, Winter 1959
16 *ibid*, Spring 1961
17 Kimber, op cit, *p 91; The Halton Magazine*, Autumn 1962
18 *The Halton Magazine*, Spring 1966
19 *ibid*, Autumn 1960
20 *ibid*, Summer 1969
   AUTHOR'S NOTE In response to his caddy's comment on a lengthy putt 'That was a lucky shot!' Gary Player replied 'Funny thing, the more I practice the luckier I become.'
21 *ibid*, Autumn 1969
22 *ibid*, The Apprentice: Forward or Backwards, Summer 1981
23 *Dateline RAF*, No 34

24   Armitage, op cit: Kimber, op cit, pp 91/92
      RAF Halton Information Yearbook (1973)
25   'RAF Halton', AHB5, 12.12.1956
26   Kimber; op cit, pp 91/92; *The Haltonian*, Summer 1983; *ibid*, Summer
      1992 (N. R. L. Ackerley); *ibid*, Winter 1988 (Ben Brown)
28   *The Haltonian*, Winter 1985
29   *ibid*, Winter 1985
30   *ibid*, Winter 1988
31   *ibid*, Winter 1989
32   *ibid*, Summer 1993

126

APPENDIX A

COMMANDANTS AND STATION COMMANDERS
RAF HALTON (1919-1993) AND RAF CRANWELL (1920-1926)

Air Vice-Marshal F R Scarlett CB DSO	1919-1924
Air Vice-Marshal C L Lambe CB CMG	1924-1928
Air Commodore C M Bonham-Carter CB OBE	1928-1931
Air Vice-Marshal N D MacEwen CMG DSO	1931-1934
Air Commodore J T Babington CBE DSO	1935-1936
Air Commodore G R M Reid DSO MC	1936-1938
Air Commodore G B Dacre CBE DSO	1938-1939
Air Vice-Marshal Sir Oliver Swann KCB CBE	1939-1940
Air Commodore G B Dacre CBE DSO	1940-1942
Air Commodore H G White CBE	1942-1946
Air Commodore J F Titmus CBE	1946-1949
Air Commodore N Carter CB DFC	1949-1951
Air Commodore J G Elton CBE DFC AFC	1951-1952
Air Commodore J G W Weston CB OBE	1952-1954
Air Commodore G N E Tindal-Carill-Worsley CB CBE	1954-1956
Air Commodore E D McK Nelson CB ADC	1956-1958
Air Commodore T N Coslett CB OBE	1958-1961
Air Commodore B Robinson CBE	1961-1963
Air Commodore D M Strong CB AFC	1963-1966
Air Commodore A C Deere DSO OBE DFC	1966-1967
Air Commodore H P Connolly CB DFC AFC AFM ADC	1967-1968
Air Commodore R H G Weighill CBE DFC ADC	1968-1973
Air Commodore B Hamilton OBE DFC AFC MRAeS MBIM	1973-1975
Air Commodore M P Stanton CBE	1975-1977
Group Captain J P Downes ADC	1977-1979
Group Captain O J Truelove MBE	1979-1981
Group Captain M J Evans ADC	1981-1983
Group Captain S R Parsons OBE CEng MRAeS	1983-1984
Group Captain R H Kyles MBE BSc(Eng) CEng MRAeS	1984-1986

Group Captain S M Williamson-Noble
MA MS CEng MRAeS   1986-1988
Group Captain I R Blunt IEng MRAeS   1988-1993
Group Captain R Brumpton MA FRAeS   1991-1993
Group Captain G O Burton   1993

ROYAL AIR FORCE HALTON

The following eight officers were Air Officer Commanding RAF Halton, an important command in its own right between the wars. Five of them had been pilots in the Royal Naval Air Service. In the words of Andrew Adam – to whose book *Beechwoods and Bayonets* the reader is recommended for fuller information – these gentlemen were a spirited and lively bunch and deserve to be remembered.

1921-1924 Air Vice-Marshal F R Scarlett CB DSO

An ex-Dartmouth cadet who had first flown in 1913, he served with the Royal Naval Air Service; one RNAS appointment was Inspecting Captain of Aircraft (ICA). As ICA, he was so dogmatic and forceful that the letters were popularly interpreted as meaning 'I can't agree'. His DSO was awarded for leading a bombing raid and fighting a German formation 'with not so much as a pistol on board'. Following his transfer to the RAF in 1918, he commanded RAF Middle East before retiring in 1931, he died in 1934.

1924-1928 Air Vice-Marshal C L Lambe CB CMG

Also ex-Royal Navy, he commanded the RNAS station at Dunkirk during World War I. After the war was Director of Equipment Air Ministry. Following Halton, he was AOC Coastal Command. He retired in 1931, and died in 1953. The obituary notice in *The Aeroplane*, ignoring his RAF career, observed that Charles Lambe was the sort of naval officer who has made the Navy what it is!

1928-1931 Air Commodore I. M. Bonham-Carter CB OBE

For a full description of this unusual and legendary figure, readers are referred to Chapter 6.

1931-1934 Air Vice-Marshal Sir Norman MacEwen CMG DSO

Born in 1881, as an Argyll and Sutherland Highlander, he fought with gallantry in the Boer War. He joined the RFC as a major in 1916. In 1919 he was appointed C-in-C RAF India. On leaving Halton he became Commandant of the Central Flying School, where he was described as 'a charming mingling of benignity and discipline'. MacEwen retired at his own request and died in 1953.

1935-1936 Air Commodore J T Babington CBE DSO

Born in 1891, following Osborne and Dartmouth he became a Midshipman in

1908. As a sub-lieutenant in 1913 he flew a Short seaplane in the first successful wireless trials at sea. In 1914 as one of three RNAS pilots, after a flight of 250 miles 'in their frail Avro with its humble horse power' (80 hp *Gnome* engines) he was awarded the DSO for successfully bombing the Zeppelin sheds at Friedrichaven while under gunfire. Promoted Air Marshal and knighted in 1942, he retired in 1942 and died in 1979.

1936-1938 Air Commodore G R M Reid DSO MC

The reader is referred to Air Cdre Reid's Foreword to this book written for me in 1981, and Chapter 5. Also an Argyll and Sutherland Highlander, Reid, after secondment to the RFC, served in France. Following Halton – where he had previously served from 1921 to 1923 – and after handling the difficult task of expanding it from a three-wing to a five-wing school of technical training – he was promoted AVM. He subsequently commanded RAF Aden and then RAF West Africa. Knighted in 1945, he retired the following year and died in 1984.

1938-1939 and 1940-1942 Air Commododre G B Dacre CBE DSO

Born in 1891, Dacre was the only officer to be twice AOC at Halton. After reading engineering at Bristol University he became a pilot in 1911. Joining the RNAS in 1914, he won the DSO at Gallipoli 'for sinking a Turkish vessel while taxying towards it under rifle fire' with an aerial torpedo. Dacre was captured and was a POW for the remainder of the war. After holding several commands between wars, he commanded the Advanced Air Striking Force of ten bomber squadrons, but returned to Halton in 1940. He retired before the war ended and died in 1962.

1939-1940 Air Vice-Marshal Sir Oliver Swann KCB CBE

Born in 1878, as a pre-war Naval Officer he purchased an Avro biplane for £700 and after fitting prototype floats became the first British pilot to take off (with 'belly-flop' landing) from salt water. While flying a German *Mars* aircraft during the war he made a forced landing on Scarborough race course. With his unfamilar uniform, German markings on the aircraft, and Germanic family name 'Commander Oliver Schwann' on his papers he was nearly shot by 'trigger-happy army recruits'. As Captain Swann, in 1915 he commanded HMS *Campania* a Cunarder vessel fitted out as an aircraft carrier with a dozen float planes. After transfer to the RAF in 1918, this time as Brigadier General, he became Deputy Chief of Air Staff. After service as Member for Personnel on the Air Staff, and AOC RAF Middle East, he retired in 1929. He was recalled to become AOC Halton on the outbreak of war. He died in 1948.

ROYAL AIR FORCE CRANWELL (1920-1926)*

The following Commandants of RAF Cranwell were responsible for the cadets of the RAF College as well as the Boy Mechanics and later Aircraft Apprentices of No 2 School of Technical Training (Boys). The education of these mechanical engineering entries (engines or airframes), as distinct from the subsequent wireless and electrical apprentice entries, closely followed that of No 1 School of Technical Training RAF Halton. In August 1926, the six Cranwell entries (Nos 1 to 6), which had become No 4 (Apprentices) Wing, moved en bloc to RAF Halton to continue training as No 4 Wing Halton.

1920-1923 Air Commodore C A H Longcraft CMG DSO AFC

Following Sandhurst, Longcraft learned to fly in 1912 and after attachment to the Air Battalion of the Royal Engineers transferred to the RFC. In 1913 when the whole of No 2 Squadron was moved by air from Farnborough to Montrose, Longcraft's BE2 made a forced landing. He passed the night in a nearby lunatic asylum which certain of his contemporaries thought to be a suitable resting place! After commanding No 4 Squadron in France and later No 2 Wing, in 1920 Longcraft, now Air Commodore, became the first Commandant of RAF Cranwell. Present at his dining out from Cranwell in 1929 were several members of his original staff including Wing Commander C F A Portal. After service as AOC Inland Area – and shortly after the departure of Trenchard – he retired in 1930 at his own request as Air Vice Marshal and was knighted in 1938.

1923-1926 Air Commodore A E Borton CB CMG DSO AFC

Following Eton, and via the Militia, 'Biffy' Borton was commissioned in the Black Watch in 1906. After learning to fly while on leave he graduated from the Central Flying School in 1914. He was wounded in France in 1915 while serving with No 8 Squadron. In 1917 he commanded the Fifth Wing in Palestine where he had close contacts with Col T. E. Lawrence whom he later met as Aircraftsman Shaw at RAF Cranwell – the College Library possesses Borton's proof copy of *The Seven Pillars of Wisdom*. After several memorable long distance flights, from December 1919 to January 1921 he served at No 1 School of Technical Training (Boys) Halton, an experience which undoubtedly proved invaluable when in 1923 he became Commandant RAF Cranwell. Promoted Air Commodore in 1922, Borton retired in 1933 by which time he was AOC Inland Area.

1926-1929 Air Commodore F C Halaham CMG CBE DSO MVO

After service in the Royal Navy beginning with HMS Britannia in 1894,

---

*See E B Haslam, *The Commandants of the Royal Air Force College Cranwell*, 1982.

Halahan specialized in gunnery. He learned to fly in 1915 by which time he was a Wing Commander in the RNAS. Transferring to the RAF in 1919 as Group Captain, he became Director of Aeronautical Inspection, and in 1924 Director of Technical Development. This experience served him well on his appointment to command RAF Cranwell. Retiring in 1930, he again served during the war before finally retiring in 1944.

APPENDIX B

THE QUEEN'S COLOUR

The highest award that a Sovereign can bestowe upon a Service formation or unit is the award of a Colour. King George VI gave his approval on 27 December 1947 to the award of colours to the Royal Air Force, the Royal Air Force College Cranwell, and No 1 School of Technical Training Royal Air Force Halton. The Colour reproduces the badge of No 1 School of Technical Training, a symbolic tree of learning derived from the beech trees in the adjacent woods and the motto *Crescentes Discimus* (As we grow, we learn).

Following the presentation of the King's (now Queen's) Colour to the Royal Air Force at Hyde Park in 1951, the Queen's Colour was presented to No 1 School of Technical Training by Her Majesty Queen Elizabeth at a parade of 1,700 apprentices at Halton on 25 July 1952. Present on this occasion were two Marshals of the Royal Air Force, Lord Trenchard and Sir John Slessor and other senior officers. At the conclusion of the dedication service, H.M. the Queen, after receiving the Colour from the Commandant of RAF Halton, Air Cdre J. G. W. Weston, made the presentation, Sgt App F M A Hines being appointed Colour Bearer to receive it. The instant of the Queen's handing over of her Colour to Sgt App Hines featured for several years at the bottom corner of the opening to British Movietone News.[1]

In her address Her Majesty said that Halton owed 'its existence to the foresight and inspiration of Lord Trenchard . . . Your traditions have been well and firmly established by those who have gone before you. For they have made their mark and have justified the confidence which the Royal Air Force has always placed in them, while many of their number have given their lives in carrying out their duties.' She concluded by saying 'I congratulate you on your drill and on the smartness of your turnout . . .' The Escort Squadron composed of the 63rd Entry to Halton then marched past in both slow and quick time. Finally the whole parade advanced in review order to give a royal salute followed by three cheers for Her Majesty before marching off.[2]

Replacement Colours were subsequently presented by HRH Princess Margaret in 1968 (Parade Commander, Flt Sgt App E J Wyer) and again by

RAF Cosford Colour Party after receiving the Colour at RAF Halton.

Colour being marched past the Halton contingent, who are presenting arms. This was the final part of the parade.

HRH The Duke of Kent in 1990 (Parade Commander, Sgt App A Burns). In his address HRH referred to this occasion marking the 70th anniversary of No 1 School of Technical Training and also to the unique tradition that allowed the Colour to be paraded by Apprentices. The Editor of the Haltonian, Bill Kelley (55th), who was also 'on parade' has recorded his one lasting impression. Despite the overall smartness and precision, it was one of 'quietness' – no crash of boots or rifle butts, and even the flypast with the environmentally friendly *Toscanos* and their whispering turbo-props failed to break the quiet of the Chiltern Hills. The only sound during the parade, apart from the bands, came from the boots and spurs of the Duke of Kent's Equerry as he accompanied His Royal Highness on his inspection.

The Queen's Colour has been proudly paraded by RAF Apprentices on many State occasions including the Queen's Silver Jubilee Royal Review of the Royal Air Force on 29 July 1977, and during Her Majesty's visit to RAF Halton on 18 July 1980 for the 60th Anniversary of Trenchard's Apprenticeship Scheme.

1 *The Haltonian*, Summer 1990 (Dave Thorman)
2 *Flight*, 1.8.1952
3 *The Haltonian*, Winter 1990

APPENDIX C

PERSONAL DIARY EXTRACTS 1938/1939
A/A Paul Tunbridge

RAF HALTON: No 1 Wing, C Squadron
January 1938-December 1939

JANUARY 1938

Friday Jan 7   *Workshops this morning and inspection this afternoon, still feel a bit homesick, am getting to bed early tonight. Soon on rigging.*

Saturday Jan 8   *Went to schools this morning. Exam coming on Monday.*

Tuesday Jan 11   *We had squad drill for first time this term.*

Monday Jan 17   *Went to rigging shop today spent all my time working the controls of several types of plane.*

Tuesday Jan 18   *Charge of improperly dressed heard, and got 3 extra duties. (No tie under greatcoat.)*

Thursday Jan 20   *Rigging again this morning am getting the hang of things now. Played hockey this afternoon 1-1. Did room job in evening.*

Saturday Jan 29   *There was a terrific storm last night in which a Boer War Memorial, a landmark, got struck by lightning.*

Wednesday Feb 9   *PT before breakfast, which isn't at all bad really. Workshops in morning, fencing in afternoon which is good fun. Library in evening.*

Thursday Feb 10	*Schools in morning, rigging in afternoon. Read in evening. Cleaned up, etc.*
Friday Feb 11	*Got confined for weekend for having a dirty locker.*
Saturday Mar 18	*We moved our boxes to prelim engines.*
Wednesday Mar 23	*Dismantling Gypsy 1 engine – think I've got the hang of it now.*
Friday Mar 25	*Pay day. Also AOC's inspection. Everybody working hard. Everything spotless.*
Saturday Mar 30	*Engines in morning. Valve timing of Gypsy 1. AOC's rehearsal in morning.*
Friday Apr 1	*Press photographers visit Halton.*
Saturday Apr 2	*Confined for weekend with dirty locker – supposed to be, was to have gone to Aylesbury.*
Tuesday Apr 5	*Inspected by AOC and Air-Vice Marshal.*
Thursday Apr 7	*Halton show 'Slipstream' in evening.*
Monday Apr 25	*Schools in morning. In afternoon we went to Chalet and kicked stones into heaps.*
Sunday May 15	*AOC's [church parade] in morning. Damn good band. Felt proud to be in RAF.*
Tuesday May 16	*Schools in morning. Stone picking seems to be finished.*
Saturday May 28	*Empire Air Day. Ran our engine in afternoon, really enjoyed myself.*
Wednesday Jun 1	*Shops in morning. Cricket in afternoon. Rained all evening, nothing to do ! Am browned off.*
Sunday Jun 19	*Church parade in morning. Secretary of State inspected us in morning. Played tennis in afternoon.*
Saturday Jul 2	*Parents' Day*

Tuesday Jul 26   *32nd Entry passed out this morning.*

Tuesday Aug 23   *Shops all morning. Rugger in afternoon got kicked several times but enjoyed it.*

Wednesday Nov 23 *Went to Henlow with Station fencing team.*

JANUARY 1939

Thursday Jan 5   *Tidied up in evening after day's work felt naturally browned off. Read 'Red Cloud Speaks'.*

Wednesday Jan 11 *Fencing in afternoon. Been doing a bit of reading recently.*

Thursday Jan 19   *Shops all day. Received 'Flying Fury'.*

Friday Jan 13   *B[ullshit] in evening.*

Friday Jan 27   *Messing Committee in afternoon – quite a scrounge.*

Friday Feb 10   *Schools. Messing Committee in afternoon, Flt Sgt gave me a fag.*

Wednesday Mar 1   *Uxbridge for fencing early in morning* [RAF Apprentices contest]. *Got on quite well.*

Tuesday Mar 7   *Fenced in afternoon. Listened to wireless in evening read "My Flying Life", Kingsford Smith.*

Monday Mar 13   *Fenced in evening against 3 Wing. I won my 3 fights.*

Sunday Mar 19   *Church parade morning. Sent postal order to Aviation Book Club.*

Wednesday Mar 22 *Fenced in afternoon. Wrote for hydraulics book from Dowtys [Mar 27 – very good book]*

Friday Mar 31   *AOC's rehearsal this afternoon. Saw Halton Show – 3 plays which were good.*

Monday May 8   *First day aerodrome. Worked on Battle*

Monday Jun 5   *Aerodrome ran up Battle, not bad fun*

Wednesday Jun 7   *Aldershot Tattoo in evening got back at 3 am*

Monday Jun 13   *Tennis in afternoon.*

Thursday Jun 22   *Aerodrome. Started Hart on compressor. B- in evening.*

Thursday Jun 29   *Shops all day. Did some more running up in morning, took the Hart up to 1400 revs.*

Saturday Jul 1   *Parents' Day. Haircut at Aston Clinton – worst haircut for a long while.*

Wednesday Jul 5   *PT in afternoon for over an hour – have fears for my locks.*

Thursday Jul 13   *Best blue inspection in afternoon. Thought it was for haircut at first.*

Monday Jul 17   *Rumours say passing out in February 1940.*

Thursday Jul 20   *F/O Evans told me we were officially passing out. I might say it was one of the happiest moments of my life.*

Saturday Jul 22   *Intermediate finishes. Science and maths today. Did better than expected.*

Saturday Aug 26   *Took things easy all day after camouflaging dugouts in morning. Looks like war.*

Saturday Sep 2   *Confined to camp in afternoon war looks imminent.*

Sunday Sep 3   *Listened to wireless at 11.15 a.m. in NAAFI, war declared – chaps cheered.*

Monday Sep 4   *Did sandbagging all day. Was damn tired when finished.*

Thursday Sep 7   *Three blue lights in evening to see with.*

Friday Sep 8   *Went on fatigues in evening after workshops all day. Long hours are getting me down.*

Monday Sep 11   *Started squadron servicing course repairing inner mainplanes of Hurricane – fabric work.*

Monday Sep 18   *35th entry passed out at 6.30 in morning.*

Friday Oct 6   *Shops all day. Nothing very exciting, not that there ever is. I don't mind where I'm posted when I leave here as long as I get out of it all.*

Tuesday Oct 10   *Components course. All theoretical but very restful.*

Friday Oct 20   *Having to wear oilskins on back and goggles on glengarry.*

Tuesday Oct 24   *Did some general studies in evening. Weighed off Singapore.*

Monday Oct 30   *Schools in morning. Went to lecture in evening 'Why Germany went to war' which was fairly good.*

Wednesday Nov 1   *Rifle drill in afternoon. Guard practice – quite amusing and was a change.*

Saturday Nov 11   *Armistice Day. Was on sandbagging all morning and just observed silence, knocked off 11 am*

Tuesday Nov 14   *Shops all day. Sandbagging in morning.*

Friday Dec 1   *18th birthday – got smoking pass. Had letter from home with cake and money.*

Wednesday Dec 13 *Passed out at 4.30 am in morning arrived at 13 Maintenance Unit, Henlow at 10 o'clock.*

APPENDIX D

EDUCATION AND TRAINING

Although there were changes in technical trade training, essentially the basic education format at Halton remained little changed until the late 'sixties. One major factor affecting the RAF apprenticeship scheme was the raising of the school leaving age. Most apprentices arriving at Halton had left school in their fourth year of secondary education prior to sitting 'O' levels or the School Leaving Certificate. Halton then functioned as a military boarding school providing education up to second year sixth form levels. About 25% of the entries gained a formal educational qualification and numbers went on to study for ground engineers' licences or qualifications either with the Royal Aeronautical Society or the Engineering Institutions. The Halton Branch of the Royal Aeronautical Society formed in 1929 'to promote and encourage interest in all branches of aeronautical science' has always flourished at Halton.

By the 1980's apprentices joining Halton were already well qualified and some 25% graduated with an Ordinary National Certificate which became the Technician Education Council Higher Certificate. In the 'eighties following the introduction of modern systems and aircraft such as the *Tornado* and the *Nimrod Mks* 2 and 3 it became increasing evident that the electrical and mechanical aspects of aircraft engineering were intimately related.[1]

Aeronautical engineering standards at No 1 School of Technical Training, RAF Halton have always been of the highest standard. Whether in workshops or schools the qualifications of instructional staff have been second to none. In the creation of an apprentice scheme on which the engineering future of the Air Force would depend, Trenchard was ably assisted by Colonel Ivor Curtis, CBE, MA, AMIMechE, Educational Adviser to the Air Ministry from 1918 until his death in 1928.[2]

As far back as 1926, in a lecture to the Royal Aeronautical Society, Wg Cdr C D Breese announced that the Halton training was now recognized by the Institution of Mechanical Engineers for those apprentices obtaining 60% in schools subjects as automatically qualifying for their student membership examination. He added that the idea that an apprentice spent most of his time learning drill was a complete fallacy. The RAF had been obliged to train its own ground engineers because aircraft companies took five years to form their own limited number of mechanics. In the RAF there were 3,000 apprentices under training ensuring an output of 1,000 a year.

The essence of Air Force training was to produce airmen able to maintain and repair many different types of aircraft and engines. To do this they had to have a thorough knowledge of the principles of construction, assembly and operation of many different units. This was in contrast to civilian training which most often was of a highly specialized nature and confined to one particular process or type of machine. Hand in hand with workshop training, educational courses were designed to provide a fundamental knowledge of mechanics, heat, electricity and magnetism, intended to lead to advanced courses on the internal combustion engine, properties and strengths of materials, theory of structures and theory of flight. To do this 8 hours a week were allocated for engineering drawing, general studies (history, literature, etc) science and mathematics.

From the outset the boy was taught to read from blueprints and working drawings and also to make personal rough sketches of the work. The first year's work enabled him to assimilate the higher courses during the remainder of the course. At the end of the first year practical and written examinations were held with a view to elimination of those unable to reach the necessary standards. Card records showing the apprentice's progress in the workshops made up at three-weekly intervals recorded his industry, practical ability, hours lost, and the results of intermediate *vive voce* examinations.

Each entry of 160 to 200 apprentices constructed three or four aircraft direct from the blueprints with timber being cut from the raw material. Jigs were made for rib construction, bending of parts, etc. Each part carried the name of the apprentice who made it and the time taken. Apprentices were very proud of their aircraft which exactly complied with the relevant specifications. Although not flown they were used for rigging instruction. On the practical and applied science instruction the school had an engine laboratory equipped with experimental engines, oil and fuel testing apparatus, cooling plant, etc. Two materials laboratories contained apparatus for conducting tests on metals and woods including impact and hardness tests. Metallurgical equipment was installed for the heat treament of aircraft materials. All the educational staff were university graduates. Two inspections had been carried out by a panel of inspectors from the Technological Department of the Board of Education, the first at Cranwell and more recently at Halton. The inspectors had recorded their 'ardent approval' of the value of this scheme of training. The system at Halton was designed to give an apprentice confidence in his knowledge and ability, as well as to promote reliability, accuracy in the use of tools, as well as reasoning power and initiative.

In the discussion on the paper, which included the points raised by a number of Halton instructional staff, Gp Capt R Peel Ross insisted on the fact that wireless was not one of the minor trades as had been suggested by the speaker. They were very proud of this specialization at Flowerdown where training was much on the same lines as at Halton and where their 300 apprentices were being passed out at the rate of 100 a year. There was one difference, however, in that training as wireless operator, wireless mechanic and electrician ran concurrently through the practical and educational sides and not from section to section. In contrast with Halton, periods of instruction were limited to one hour each on a particular subject following which the apprentices moved on to something else.

Lt Col W Lockwood Marsh spoke of the thoroughness of the engineering training and general education training given at Halton shown by the fact that 12 [sic] boys annually could go on from Halton to Cranwell for training as officer cadets. There they did extremely well, the Sword of Honour that year had gone to an apprentice from Halton and the previous year two had passed out top. This was great testimony to the extraordinarily efficient training at Halton.

He strongly advocated a separate engineering branch in the Royal Air Force such as in the old days in both the RNAS and RFC. The King's Regulations stipulated that in each squadron a 'properly qualified officer', denoted by an 'E' after their name, should be in charge of the workshops. This was not the case, for after spending four days checking through the relevant lists he had found that out of 43 squadrons only eight had an 'E' specialist on their strength. Furthermore in these eight squadrons, three of the 'E' specialists were the commanding officers themselves!

Colonel Curtis, who had been associated with Halton training from the outset, recalled that in 1919 when the manning of the new Air Force was under consideration there existed a school of thought that education was of no use to the practical man, and was even a disadvantage. Their six years' experience at Halton had served largely to dispel this view. Education was an important part of Halton training and 70% of the entrants were from secondary and technical schools. The continuance of that education throughout the apprenticeship would produce a by-product of men of very high ability. The question for the future was what use should be made of this exceptional product. It was for this reason both at Flowerdown and Halton that apart from the technical side they were endeavouring to give a wide general education. Colonel Sempill, on the other hand, considered that one disadvantage arising from the great importance paid to education was that the system would appear to be more suitable for the production of officers. This factor in itself could cause a good deal of dissatisfaction unless promotion from the ranks was higher than now appeared to be the case.

Wg Cdr Breese in reply to a question on possible Trade Union recognition said that no boys trained under the system had as yet completed their ten years service. He estimated that about 7% of the 30,000 mechanics in the RAF had been trained at Halton. He agreed on the desirability of a technical officer branch and that provision for this would probably be met in part by Halton trained cadets...because they would have had three years sound technical training at Halton as well as a subsequent two years officers' training at Cranwell. In fact, as mentioned elsewhere, the RAF Technical Branch which came into existence only in July 1939 did not become functional until July 1940.[3]

Lt Col A F S Caldwell, DSO, MA who was Principal of the School from October 1926 to August 1932, founded the Old Haltonians Society on 19 November 1925 to enable ex-apprentices to keep in touch by arranging reunions and to provide help for them during or after their RAF service.

Another early member of the teaching staff, Captain A B Fanshawe, AFC, MA, was first editor of the *Halton Magazine* in 1924 and who that year also founded the Halton Debating Society. This, in 1933 blossomed into the Halton Society whose activities by 1937 included art, aero-engineering, model aircraft, cycling, radio and wireless, philately, etc. Fanshawe's educational career embraced RAF Cranwell and Cosford and finally war service in North America with the aircrew training scheme until his retirement in 1946. In his message to RAF Halton in 1945 on the occasion of the Silver Jubilee celebration of the Trenchard Apprentice Scheme Fanshawe wrote:

> '. . . Halton surely can show a finer Roll of Honour than any other military training school in the world. And that is no figure of speech...Ex-apprentices form the hard core of the Royal Air Force and fortunately one finds them in every unit. One of my flight commanders is an ex-apprentice . . . and I would not change him for anyone. My Commanding Officer is one of my old ex-apprentices and daily I salute him with pride . . . But what thrills me most about these apprentices is that they are all proud to have started as apprentices and that they frankly attribute their progress to their thorough training . . . which make the British airman the envy of our Allies and the despair of our foes . . .' [4]

In pre-war years, as part of the general studies course, apprentices selected a 'set task' from a choice of given subjects. These set tasks, submitted in booklet form complete with maps, illustrations and references were often of a very high standard, and continued to form part of the Halton educational syllabus up to about 1938 when the need to compress courses made this impracticable.

I remember one corporal apprentice of the 32nd entry in 1938 proudly showing me his set task entitled 'Petroleum' which included descriptions and diagrams of operating and refining processes, and distribution channels – the whole illustrated with photographs obtained from several oil companies constituted a comprehensive booklet.

Another apprentice, A L Holland of the 17th entry, recalls that after reading every book in the well-stocked Halton Library and articles on rigid airships, published in the Royal Aeronautical Society's Journals, he chose as subject in 1930 'Lighter than air craft'. One of the workshop instructors who had been a 'Rigger Balloon' gave him assistance on the operational aspects of balloons.

One autumn morning Holland, who had just sounded reveillé on his trumpet, was surprised to see 'the beautiful silver pencil with gracefully rounded prow and stern of the R101 as her course took her just clear of our wooded Chiltern hills above 1 and 2 Wings'. The R101 subsequently crashed on a hillside in France.[5]

The Halton Society sponsored numbers of comic operas and plays in the 1930's, produced with the enthusiastic support of A C Kermode. A.C.K., as he was generally known, was the author of *Principles of Flight*, while his colleague J Haddon wrote the companion volumes *Structures*, and also *Properties and strengths of materials*, published in 1931, all three volumes ran into several editions.

A.C.K. had qualified as an RNAS pilot at HMS *Daedulus* (Cranwell) in 1916 when, following distinguished war service, he had joined the RAF Educational Service as a civilian which offered scope for his genius in teaching and his passionate enthusiasm for flying. He served again at Cranwell in the early days of the apprentice scheme before proceeding to Halton where he remained until 1936, when for the third time he returned to Cranwell as senior tutor in aeronatutical science and engineering at the RAF Cadet College. At the outbreak of war, he became Chief Ground Instructor at the Empire Flying School, and in 1946 he was made responsible for co-ordinating the whole instructional plan on the reopening of the Cadet College Cranwell.[6]

Wg Cdr Kimber, beneath a fine portrait of Air Vice-Marshal A C Kermode CBE, MA, FRAeS, whose final appointment was head of the RAF Education Branch, wrote: '*Son of Halton* is dedicated to his memory and all those who layered the mortar and built the superstructure to Lord Trenchard's foundation . . .'

The Kermode Memorial Prize awarded at Halton for many years (the last recorded prizewinner was R B Lee, 131st entry, reported in *The Haltonian* 1981) commemorated his outstanding contribution to the education of Halton apprentices. Captain Fanshawe wrote of 'the amazing personality of A.C.K., author, pilot, poet, playwright, producer and, in the classroom, prince of pedagogues and apprentices' friend . . .'

The education service was fully integrated into the RAF in 1946 at about the same time as the introduction of the Educational and Vocational Training (EVT) scheme. Much of the educational success at Halton stemmed from the untiring efforts of 'Old Kermode'. A farewell message, perhaps more hopeful than poetical, to the first Halton entry which passed out in 1924 was signed A.C.K. [Kermode]:

> Your time is up – your fate is sealed – and now
> You leave us with a sense of splendid pride;
> First in the field, to you the honour falls
> To spread the name of Halton far and wide.

Where'er you go, remember this:
You will be watched – Yes, some perhaps may try
To trip you up, to run your training down;
With you alone it rests to show they lie.

Others will want to see what you are worth,
To test your knowledge, commonsense and skill:
Will you respond? Will you come up to scratch?
As we at Halton hope and trust you will.

Entries to follow, be they good or bad,
Cannot attain what's yours and yours alone-
The privilege will never come again,
You were the first – the only – Number One.
Troubles you had – what pioneers had not?
But commonsense – a pair of hands – and pluck,
Will take you far; so barracks, shops and school
Do wish you all the very best of luck.[7]

1 *The Haltonian*, Summer 1981
2 Kimber, op cit, p 82
3 Wg Cdr C. D. Bresse AFC, 'The training of aircraft apprentices', *Journal of the RAeSoc*, March 1927
4 Kimber, op cit, reproduced on p 118
5 *The Haltonian*, Summer 1991
6 *Journal of the Royal Air Force College*, Winter 1948
7 *The Haltonian*, Summer 1982 (Air Cdre Dicken: 5th entry).
   Journal of the RAF College, Winter 1948 and Kimber, op cit

APPENDIX E

THE HALTON AERO CLUB

The Halton Aero Club (HAC) founded by the School staff came into existence in December 1925 at a time when there were only two other flying clubs. Inter-club competitions took place in which club-built light aeroplanes participated. Designed and constructed by local enthusiasts, such planes could not compete with those manufactured by aircraft companies in the early 'thirties when many amateur clubs closed down. The Halton Aero Club (HAC) existed until December 1930 when it became the Halton Aeronautical Society, a branch of the Royal Aeronautical Society, one of the offshoots of the multifarious activities of the Halton Society.

The main purpose of the Club was to design and construct a light aircraft, the HAC1 *Mayfly* – obviously someone thought it 'may not' – for flying in inter-club competitions. Its first flight in January 1927 was reported in *Flight* under the comment 'The Mayfly does'. The name 'may-fly' was chosen because this insect of the Ephemeropta order has a flying life of only a few days following several years in an immature stage. This fact was mentioned in the Summer 1928 number of *The Halton Magazine*.

Designed by C H Latimer-Needham FRAeS whose flying experience dated back to the RFC, his subsequent career included design, construction and experimental test flying. He was Chief Engineer of Flight Refuelling Ltd in the late 1940's/early 1950's. Also prominent in the design of the two-seater biplane were Halton education officers, A C Kermode (Hon Secretary of the Halton Aero Club), H L Collis and Flt Lt Hart aided by civilian instructors. Some had said the machine would never be built; that if it were built it would never fly; if it did fly it would break the pilot's neck!

Contributions towards the £300 cost of building *Mayfly* came from the 1,100 members of the Halton Aero Club on the basis of five shilling or half-crown (for Aircraft Apprentices) shares. Many apprentice shareholders had left Halton before the maiden flight.

The *Mayfly* was built in 1926-27 by two hundred carpenter-riggers of the January 1924 Entry mainly in their free time, although some apprentices were

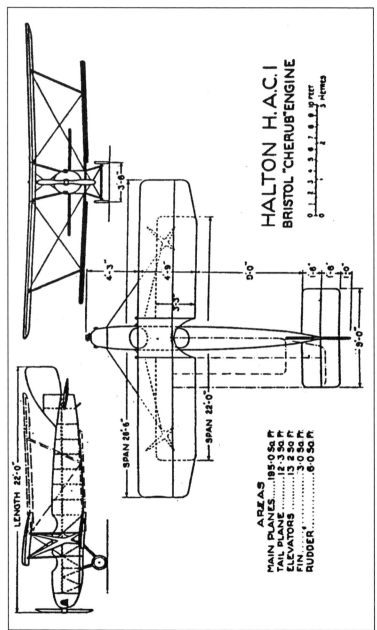

HALTON H.A.C.I
BRISTOL "CHERUB" ENGINE

ARLAS
MAIN PLANES........195·0 Sq. Ft.
TAIL PLANE ....12·3 Sq. Ft.
ELEVATORS ....13 2 Sq. Ft.
FIN ....3·0 Sq. Ft.
RUDDER.................6·0 Sq. Ft.

LENGTH 22·0"

SPAN 26·6"

SPAN 22·0"

The Halton HAC 1 Mayfly designed and built at RAF Halton. The Halton HAC 2 Minus was the monoplane version of the HAC 1 after shedding its lower wings.

(Courtesy of Aeroplane Monthly.)

permitted to make certain structural parts of the plane as part of their training. Originally a two-seater (the C of A No 1278 shows date of registration 23 June 1926) the plane was converted to a single-seater (retaining the same registration number G-EBOO) and a Certificate of Airworthiness issued on 13 May 1927. The *Mayfly* was the subject of a contribution to *The Halton Magazine* by the amazing Kermode (A.C.K.) which recounts the three stages of the development of the aircraft:

THE SCHOOL – JANUARY 1926

> What! only a mass of figures,
> Equations, logs and sines,
> Page after page of symbols,
> And intersecting lines;
> What use these strange devices
> Which make my blood to freeze?
> Good sir, my frank advice is,
> Have no concern with these!
> I admire your mathematics,
> But I doubt, I know not why,
> If an aeroplane built of figures
> Is ever destined to fly.

THE WORKSHOPS – JULY 1926

> What! only a skeleton structure
> Of wires and pieces of wood,
> Held together by nothing
> But a hope that the glue is good!
> Why dabble in things beyond you,
> And put your trade to shame ?
> Nay, carpenter, cease your fooling,
> Return to your window frame!
> I admire your skill with chisels,
> But I doubt, I know not why,
> If an aeroplane built by 'chippies'
> Is ever destined to fly.

BICESTER AERODROME – JANUARY 1927

Ah! now for the test that matters,
Now I feel more at home,
As the sound of running engines
Is wafted across the 'drome;
She's away – tail up – why, look, sir –
Great Heavens ! she's off the floor!
Good sir, you may sheathe your slide-rule,
Return your chisels to store,
For I take off my hat to 'chippies',
To maths I apologise,
It was only a mass of gigures,
But nevertheless – IT FLIES!

The dual-control machine was a tractor biplane with high gap/chord and span/chord ratios and a pronounced stagger. The plane was powered by one 32 hp Bristol *Cherub* III engine, mounted on four steel brackets, with a duralumin propeller presented to the club by the Fairey Aircraft Company. The undercarriage consisted of steel tubing fitted with rubber cord shock-absorbers.

The single-unit wing struts in the form of an unsymmetrical letter X must have created a problem for the designer and draughtsman. Additional drag bracing-wires, resulting from an error in the original wing stressing, were fitted externally to nose and tail. For simplicity, the aileron control wires and pulleys were mounted externally although originally intended to be fitted inside the wings. The flat-sided box-type fuselage had a light skeleton of spruce covered with plywood. The latter created some difficulties since plywood 'can be bent over a cylinder but not over a barrel'.

The HAC1, made its first test flight from Bicester on 31 January 1927 with Flt Lt C F le Poer Trench, a notable WWI pilot, at the controls. According to an apprentice of the 28th Entry, one of Le Poer Trench's stunts was to fly along the length of the hangar-roof with his undercarriage chassis on each side of the roof-ridge, his other stunt was, unbelievably, to fly through the hangar. According to a lengthy report in *Flight*, with an all-up weight of 920 pounds the machine responded well to the controls, had a low landing speed, cruised at 75 mph and a maximum speed of 83 mph.[1]

The plane was described in *The Aeroplane* as undoubtedly one of the finest light aeroplanes in existence. The editor of *Flight* in describing it as a very creditable piece of work hoped that it would participate in meetings and races that summer for the satisfaction of the boys who helped to produce it. In fact, during 1927 the HAC1 gained numbers of trophies and cups as well as £150 in cash prizes. These included nine first prizes with the same pilot.

During 1928 the plane now converted to a single-seater high-wing monoplane, the HAC2 *Minus*, with a maximum speed of 93 mph and reduced weight of 720 pounds, was equally successful. Again flown by Flt Lt le Poer Trench that year it won three firsts as well as the Wakefield Cup. The HAC2 was one of the leading aircraft in the fly-past at the RAF air display on 30 June. Again the following year the HAC2 gained five firsts and won the Headquarters race for the Duke of York's Cup. According to the Certificate of Airworthiness the plane (still described as '2-seater light biplane') was finally dismantled at Halton on 8 February 1931.

Meanwhile before the HAC2 was completed, Latimer-Needham, Kermode, and the design team had been at work on the HAC3 (the *Meteor*). This was an altogether different design, a tailless monoplane of two-engine design (both Bristol *Cherubs*, mounted in tandem) one tractor and the other propulsor. In the absence of airworthiness requirements for tailless aircraft of this type construction was slow. In the *Halton Magazine* of Xmas 1928 a lecture was announced for members of the Aero Club for the following February giving a description of the design of the HAC3. The airframe did not get beyond the 90% completion stage because the 15th Entry, the last entry of carpenter/riggers at Halton, passed out in 1930 leaving no-one to finish the work. It is believed that the uncompleted airframe might have been handed over to the Watford Artisans' Club. Yet another design for a six-seater, numbered HAC4, a high-wing monoplane did not get beyond the drawing-board stage.

To mark Halton's contribution to club flying, the Halton Aero Club was presented in 1929 with a light aircraft, the *Sparrow*, by the Supermarine Aero Company. The Halton Aero Club continued to exist until the end of the following year by which time it had became clear that club-built aircraft could not compete with commercially constructed aircraft. As a result, Halton's do-it-yourself building programme came to an end on 31 December 1930 at which date the Aero Club became the Halton Aeronautical Society, a branch of the Royal Aeronautical Society with a wider range of activities.

---

1 'The Fledgling' by 562270 (AHB)
Other sources:
Kimber op cit, pp 83, 114,115.
The Halton Magazine, Easter, Summer, Xmas 1927, Summer 1928.
The Haltonian, Winter 1988 ('Ali' Murch);Summer 1989 (Stanley Caffin/Dave Ashenden).
A J Jackson, *British Civil Aircraft since 1919*, Vol 2. James A Wilson's *Aircraft of the Halton Aero Club*, 1992, illustrated review. See also Chaz Bowyer, 'Halton Home-Builds', *Halton Magazine*, Summer 1971.
Flight 17.2.1927 (illustrated).
The Aeroplane, 28.12.1927
Certificate of Airworthiness

150

APPENDIX F

CADETSHIPS TO ROYAL AIR FORCE COLLEGE CRANWELL

Of the 4,383 Flight Cadets who between 1920 and 1973 passed through the RAF College Cranwell, 301 were ex-apprentices. Up to 1940, Flight Cadet entries were numbered according to the period of training, ie. 38-39 (1938-1939). There were no Cadet entries during the war; post-war entries received a separate number, in this way the three entries which began training in January 1947 were numbered 45, 46, 47. Entry Numbers with dates are shown at the end of the roll.

There were two entries a year except in 1920 when there were three (of which the first was a Naval Entry) in 1938 there were again three entries and in 1940 only one. **Only Apprentices selected for officer training at the RAF College up to 1973 are shown below. An asterisk indicates those graduates still serving in 1990 – they will all have been promoted!**

From 1938, to meet the urgent demand for pilots called for by the Air Force expansion, the duration of the usual two-year course was progressively reduced. In this way, for example, the last wartime course which had begun training in April 1940 graduated in July 1940. Following resumption of Cadet training in January 1947 (a 15-month course) the duration of the course was extended to 2 or 3 years.

The last Flight Cadet Entry No 101 graduated from the Royal Air Force College on 16 March 1973. Under the new university graduate scheme introduced in September that year entrants – who had already obtained their 'wings' – trained at the RAF College Cranwell for twelve months prior to undergoing advanced and operational training elsewhere.

Ex-Cranwell apprentice entrants up to Entry No 28-31 would have trained at No 4 Wing Cranwell as 'mechanicals' (ie mainly engine/airframes). Subsequent to 1926 (when No 4 Wing Cranwell moved *en bloc* to Halton) ex-Cranwell apprentices shown below as Flight Cadets would have been 'non-mechanicals', ie wireless and electrical, instrument makers, etc. Apprentice training in the latter category which had begun at Flowerdown in 1922 ended in 1929.

CADET ENTRY	NAME	FINAL RANK	APPRENTICE SCHOOL (Halton unless indicated)
20-22	**Dawson W L**	**Air Chief Marshal Sir Walter**	
23-25	**Cannon L W**	**Air Vice-Marshal**	Cranwell
23-25	**Coats R**	**Air Commodore**	Cranwell
23-25	**Nowell H E**	**Air Commodore**	Cranwell
23-24	O'Hanlon F S	Flt Lt	Cranwell
23-25	Worsley T E	Fg Off	Cranwell
24-26	Brake K S	Gp Capt	Cranwell
24-26	Finch E S	Gp Capt	Cranwell
24-25	**Freebody W L**	**Air Vice-Marshal**	Cranwell
24-25	**Heard C M**	**Air Commodore**	Cranwell
24-26	**Mutch J B**	**Air Commodore**	Cranwell
24-25	**Spreckley H D**	**Air Marshal Sir H**	Cranwell
24-25	Stapleton P J	Fg Off	Cranwell
24-25	Wisher H G	Wg Cdr	Cranwell
25-27	**Grierson C M**	**Air Commodore**	
25-27	Moore W M	Wg Cdr	
25-28	**Stephenson J N T**	**Air Vice-Marshal**	
26-27	Allen J E	Gp Capt	
26-27	**Field R C**	**Air Commodore**	
26-27	MacCallum J E M	Gp Capt	
26-28	**Mutch J**	**Air Commodore**	Cranwell
26-27	Proctor G H H	Gp Capt	
26-27	**Tait N A**	**Air Commodore**	
26-28	Weait A L	Fg Off	Cranwell
26-28	**Whittle F**	**Air Cdre Sir Frank**	Cranwell
26-28	**Worstall W R**	**Air Commodore**	Cranwell
27-28	Beaman W R	Gp Capt	
27-29	Crocker L	Gp Capt	
27-29	**Lane D W**	**Air Commodore**	
27-29	Lewis K P	Gp Capt	
27-29	**Phillips R L**	**Air Commodore**	Flowerdown
27-28	Rutherford J D	Gp Capt	
27-28	Shelley B T	Flt Lt	Flowerdown
27-28	Sturgiss F C	Gp Capt	Flowerdown
28-31	Angel D V	Plt Off	
28-30	Coote P B	Wg Cdr	
28-29	**Earle A**	**Air Marshal Sir Alfred**	
28-29	McKechnie W N	Gp Capt	
28-29	Sawyer W	Plt Off	
28-30	**Shirley T U C**	**Air Vice-Marshal Sir Thomas**	Flowerdown
28-29	Whitehead J	Gp Capt	

CADET ENTRY	NAME	FINAL RANK	APPRENTICE SCHOOL (Halton unless indicated)
28-29	Wicks F F	Gp Capt	Flowerdown
29-30	**Coslett T N**	**Air Marshal Sir Norman**	
29-31	Daubney F C	Gp Capt	Cranwell
29-30	Horner T Q	Gp Capt	
29-31	**Messenger A D**	**Air Commodore**	Cranwell
29-30	Nichols W T H	Gp Capt	Flowerdown
29-30	Reed W S	Gp Capt	
29-31	Rutter N C S AVM	Sqn Ldr	
29-31	**Widdows S C**	**Air Commodore**	
29-31	Williams G W	Sqn Ldr	
29-30	**Wrigley H B**	**Air Vice-Marshal**	Flowerdown
30-32	**Carter R A C**	**Air Commodore**	
30-32	Gale T G L	Sdn Ldr	
30-32	**Marchbank S J**	**Air Commodore**	
30-31	Monks R	Flt Lt	Cranwell
30-31	Porter E F	Wg Cdr	
30-31	**Pyke A**	**Air Commodore**	Cranwell
31-33	Badger J V C	Sqn Ldr	
31-33	Becker B H	Gp Capt	
31-33	**Chacksfield B A**	**Air Vice-Marshal**	
31-33	**Disbrey W D**	**Air Commodore**	
31-33	Fairweather RR	Wg Cdr	Cranwell
31-33	**Finlay D**	**Air Commodore**	
31-32	Patmore S P A	Gp Capt	
31-32	**Pope J C**	**Air Vice-Marshal**	
31-32	**Porter M K D**	**Air Marshal Sir Kenneth**	
31-32	Robinson P R	Wg Cdr	
32-33	Francis C C	Fg Off	
32-34	Kirk J E	Gp Capt	
32-33	Sanders A T D	Wg Cdr	
32-33	Thripp G	Wg Cdr	Cranwell
32-34	Yaxley R G	Gp Capt	
33-35	**Bayley J W**	**Air Commodore**	
33-34	Bicknell L C	Gp Capt	
33-35	Croce F E	Gp Capt	
33-35	Mason A J	Gp Capt	
33-35	**Melvin J D**	**Air Commodore**	
33-36	**Menaul S W B**	**Air Vice-Marshal**	Cranwell
33-34	Rose L	Gp Capt	
33-34	Vickery H C	Fg Off	
33-34	Whillier A J	Fg Off	

CADET ENTRY	NAME	FINAL RANK	APPRENTICE SCHOOL (Halton unless indicated)
34-35	Atkins A R	Wg Cdr	
34-36	Darling V C	Gp Capt	
34-36	Fishwick J R	Flt Lt	
34-36	**Warcup P E**	**Air Commodore**	
35-36	Cooper L F	Sdn Ldr	
35-37	Cox P A N	Fg Off	
35-36	Fraser J G	Wg Cdr	
35-37	Frogley R T	Gp Capt	
35-36	Milne C D	Gp Capt	
35-37	Pitcairn-Hill J A	Sdn Ldr	
35-37	Wigg P M	Sdn Ldr	Cranwell
35-37	**Wykeham P G**	**Air Marshal Sir Peter**	
36-38	**Barnard J O**	**Air Commodore**	
36-37	Hatfield P R	Wg Cdr	
36-38	Lambert P C	Wg Cdr	
36-37	**Lapsley J H**	**Air Marshal Sir John**	
36-37	Maybury D C	Fg Off	
36-38	Petre G W	Gp Capt	
36-38	Porter E O	Sqn Ldr	Cranwell
36-37	Preston T	Wg Cdr	
36-38	**Willis C V D**	**Air Commodore**	
37-39	Beringer W	Gp Capt	
37-38	Dunn H J R	Plt Off	
37-38	Harris R E	Plt Off	
37-38	**Holmes J A**	**Air Commodore**	Cranwell
37-39	Mace B G	Fg Off	
37-39	Mould P W O	Sdn Ldr	
37-38	Robertson C	Wg Cdr	
37-38	Stevens B O C	Plt Off	
37-39	Winch H J	Wg Cdr	
38-39	**Bird F R**	**Air Vice-Marshal**	
38-39	Davey J T F	Plt Off	
38-39	Light C	Plt Off	
38-39	MacDonald J M	Flt Lt	Cranwell
38-39	Nettledon P J M	Plt Off	
38-39	Padfield E W	Fg Off	
38-39	Sharman D C	Flt Lt	
38-39	Temlett C B	Flt Lt	Cranwell
38-39	Warren C	Wg Cdr	
39	Clegg B	Flt Lt	Cranwell
39	Clifford R H	Plt Off	

CADET ENTRY	NAME	FINAL RANK	APPRENTICE SCHOOL (Halton unless indicated)
39	Deas J H	Plt Off	
39-40	Plumb J A	Plt Off	Cranwell
40	Davey J A J	Plt Off	
40	Jackson E	Plt Off	Cranwell
40	Wheatley-Smith T R N	Wg Cdr	
46	Muff D J	Fg Off	
49	Armour P M	Flt Lt	
49	Ball B J	Wg Cdr	
49	Keeling P F	Fg Off	
49	Knapper W F	Gp Capt	
49	Short M	Gp Capt	Cranwell
49	Turner A	Flt Lt	
51	Broad P J	Wg Cdr	
51	Copping G	Plt Off	Cranwell
51	Jones R D	Plt Off	Cranwell
51	Murphy J N	Flt Lt	Cranwell
51	Southon V A	Flt Lt	Cranwell
51	Watson R	Gp Capt	
51	**Williamson K A**	**Sir Keith, Marshal of the RAF**	Cranwell
52	Banks E F	Gp Capt	
52	Gill M	Sdn Ldr	
52	Goatley B J	Wg Cdr	
52	Hammans G D	Fg Off	
52	Meadows J	Gp Capt	
53	Spry B A	Sdn Ldr	
53	Stevens I P	Wg Cdr	St Athan
53	**Wirdnam K A C**	**Air Commodore**	
54	Mallett K F E	Wg Cdr	
54	Wilkinson K J	Sdn Ldr	
55	Cockerill L G	Flt Lt	
55	**Gladding R E**	**Air Commodore**	Cranwell
55	Gregory E F W	Fg Off	
56	Daly J H D	Sqn Ldr	
56	Davies J R	Wg Cdr	
56	Kennet P	Flt Lt	
56	Scott A J J	Wg Cdr	Cranwell
56	Warren D H	Gp Capt	
57	**Edwards D J**	**Air Commodore**	Cranwell
57	Willis G	Sdn Ldr	
58	**Armitage**	**Air Chief Marshal Sir Michael**	
58	Boyle J S	Flt Lt	Cranwell

CADET ENTRY	NAME	FINAL RANK	APPRENTICE SCHOOL (Halton unless indicated)
58	**Fitzpatrick**	**Air Marshal Sir John**	
58	**Pack J M**	**Air Commodore**	St Athan
58	Underdown P J	Flt Lt	
59	Brand G J	Fg Off	
59	Tucker J A	Flt Lt	
60	**Allison Duncan**	**Air Commodore**	
60	Marsh M M	Flt Lt	
61	Langley J D	Flt Lt*	
61	McLeod J	Gp Capt*	
61	Spatcher J L	Sdn Ldr	
61	**Allison Dennis**	**Air Vice-Marshal**	
62	Poyser G F	Wg Cdr	
64	Hines F M A	Wg Cdr	
64	Merry J F	Sdn Ldr	St Athan
64	Papworth P M	Wg Cdr	
65	Biddiscombe P G	Sdn Ldr	Cranwell
67	Durnford H T M	Sqn Ldr	
67	McVie J	Sdn Ldr	Locking
67	Talbot G A	Sdn Ldr	
68	Hemsley S E	Flt Lt	St Athan
68	Morgan R G	Wg Cdr	St Athan
69	Hicks M A	Locking	
69	Lees J R	Sdn Ldr	
69	Seekings M R J	Flt Lt	
69	Trump P A R	Plt Off	St Athan
70	Enright T E	RNZAF	
70	Ettridge A G	Sdn Ldr	
70	Walter E J	Flt Lt	
71	Kerr R G	Sdn Ldr	Locking
71	Cottingham A S	Sqn Ldr	
73	Thomson A E	RNZAF	
75	Barrett R J	Wg Cdr*	
75	McMahon J J	Flt Lt	
78	Hallam R P	Gp Capt*	
79	Adams C J	Sqn Ldr*	Locking
79	Gibson R H	Flt Lt	
79	Jackson D R	Sdn Ldr	
81	Nottingham J	Sdn Ldr	Locking
81	Thomson R B	RNZAF	
81	Wade G N	Flt Lt	
82	Mitchell R	Sdn Ldr	

CADET ENTRY	NAME	FINAL RANK	APPRENTICE SCHOOL (Halton unless indicated)
83	Dales M	Sqn Ldr*	Locking
84	Stockley T P	Sdn Ldr	Locking
85	Mullan C J	Flt Lt	Locking
85	Pearse S	Flt Lt	
87	Rayfield G	Sqn Ldr	
87	Tyndall W F C	Flt Lt	Locking
88	Upton C E	Wg Cdr*	
89	Cooper M G	Wg Cdr*	
89	Dean M S	Sdn Ldr*	Locking
89	Denham D C	Wg Cdr*	
89	Daimondopoulos D	Wg Cdr*	
89	Gunaratnum N	Plt Off	
89	Ledsham N R	Sdn Ldr	
89	Pyle M W	Flt Lt	
89	Taylor G T	Flt Lt*	Locking
89	Thomas A R	Sdn Ldr*	
90	Coles R N	Fg Off	
90	Pyle G S	Sqn Ldr	Locking
90	Reid M	Flt Lt	
90	Sims R N S	Wg Cdr*	
91	Lynch W	Flt Lt	
91	Mitchell R A K	Sdn Ldr	
91	Sharman P B	Sdn Ldr	Locking
91	Slack R A	Sdn Ldr	
91	Wilson R L	Fg Off	
91	Withers A F	Flt Lt	
92	Brunton I A J	Flt Lt	
92	Funnell-Bailey C C	Flt Lt*	Locking
92	Marshall L J	Wg Cdr	
93	Bates J	Sdn Ldr	
93	Evans A	Sqn Ldr*	
93	Hall A V	Wg Cdr*	
93	Hollowood J W	Wg Cdr*	Locking
93	Hurst A J	Sdn Ldr	
93	Locke T F	Flt Lt	
93	Maan M H	Wg Cdr*	
93	Marcus J	Flt Lt	
93	Mullen T A F	Flt Lt*	
93	Phillips J W	Fg Off	
93	Smith G P	Wg Cdr*	
93	Weight P E	Sdn Ldr*	Locking

CADET ENTRY	NAME	FINAL RANK	APPRENTICE SCHOOL (Halton unless indicated)
93	Wildman J G	Wg Cdr*	
93	Woolstencroft S	Sdn Ldr	
94	Bate L C	Sdn Ldr*	Locking
94	Deffee P R D	Plt Off	Locking
94	Dillon J A	Flt Lt	
94	Dillon K	Sqn Ldr	
94	Dixon M	Flt Lt	Locking
94	Fuller R F	Sdn Ldr	
94	Green G N	Sqn Ldr*	
94	Hooper R W	Wg Cdr*	
94	Inge P	Sdn Ldr*	
94	Martin D A	Sqn Ldr*	
94	McLeod G	Wg Cdr*	Locking
94	Neal B R	Wg Cdr*	
94	Peele R A	Flt Lt	
94	Slawson P R	Sdn Ldr	
94	Spink C R	Gp Capt	
94	Whitear G S	Flt Lt	
94	Woodley M E	Sdn Ldr*	Locking
95	Bedford E	Flt Lt*	
95	Britton M S	Plt Off	Locking
95	Denwood V R	Sqn Ldr*	
95	Duggan T E	Sqn Ldr*	
95	Le Jeune P V	Flt Lt	
95	Pettigrew E	Flt Lt	
95	Poulter L G	Flt Lt	
95	Sloss I	Wg Cdr*	
95	Wakely B	Wg Cdr*	
95	Webb D J	Flt Lt	
96	Bairstowe G	Flt Lt*	
96	Baldwin C C	Flt Lt	
96	Bills D T	Wg Cdr*	
96	Bowden D B	Sqn Ldr	
96	Dunmore A	Flt Lt	Locking
96	Foster F W	Sqn Ldr	
96	Hodgson G F	Sdn Ldr*	
96	Housman W A	Sdn Ldr	
96	Joyner C D	Sdn Ldr*	
96	Minter P C	Sdn Ldr*	Locking
96	Neo C K	Sdn Ldr	
96	Saifurrahman Z A	Sdn Ldr	

CADET ENTRY	NAME	FINAL RANK	APPRENTICE SCHOOL (Halton unless indicated)
96	Sargent J	Flt Lt	Locking
96	Simpson W G	Wg Cdr	
96	Summers T J	Flt Lt	Locking
97	Banks D R	Flt Lt	Locking
97	Booker G S F	Wg Cdr*	
97	Burgess K J	Sqn Ldr*	Cosford
97	Cossar A K	Wg Cdr*	Cosford
97	Dorey A J	Flt Lt *	Cosford
97	Hudson D B	Sdn Ldr*	Locking
97	Hughes C E	Flt Lt	
97	McGrath W J	Sdn Ldr*	Cosford
97	Paterson G A	Wg Cdr*	Locking
98	McGuire K	Flt Lt*	Locking
98	Sharp R J	Wg Cdr*	Locking
98	Watkins R P	Plt Off	
98	Wyer E J	Sdn Ldr*	
99	Britten-Austin H G	Wg Cdr*	Locking
99	Rounds T W B	Sqn Ldr*	Locking

RAF COLLEGE ENTRY DATES

45	Jan 47	Apr 48	64	Sep 52	Apr 55	83	Sep 60	Jul 63
46	Jan 47	Apr 49	65	Jan 53	Jul 55	84	Jan 61	Dec 63
47	Jan 47	Jul 49	66	Apr 53	Dec 55	85	Sep 61	Jul 64
48	Apr 47	Dec 49	67	Sep 53	Apr 56	86	Jan 62	Dec 64
49	Sep 47	Apr 50	68	Jan 54	Jul 56	87	Sep 62	Jun 65
50	Jan 48	Jul 50	69	Apr 54	Apr 57	88	Jan 63	Dec 65
51	Apr 48	Dec 50	70	Sep 54	Jul 57	89	Sep 63	Jul 66
52	Sep 48	Apr 51	71	Jan 55	Dec 57	90	Apr 64	Mar 67
53	Jan 49	Aug 51	72	Apr 55	Apr 58	91	Oct 64	May 67
54	Apr 49	Dec 51	73	Sep 55	Jul 58	92	Mar 65	Aug 67
55	Sep 49	Dec 51	74	Jan 56	Dec 58	93	Oct 65	Mar 68
56	Jan 50	Jul 52	75	Sep 56	Jul 59	94	Mar 66	Aug 68
57	Apr 50	Dec 52	76	Jan 57	Dec 59	95	Oct 66	Feb 69
58	Sep 50	Apr 53	77	Sep 57	Jul 60	96	Mar 67	Aug 69
59	Jan 51	Jul 53	78	Jan 58	Dec 60	97	Oct 67	Feb 70
60	May 51	Dec 53	79	Sep 58	Aug 61	98	Apr 68	Jul 70
61	Sep 51	Apr 54	80	Jan 59	Dec 61	99	Sep 68	Feb 71
62	Jan 52	Jul 54	81	Sep 59	Jul 62	100	Sep 69	Feb 72
63	May 52	Dec 54	82	Jan 60	Dec 62	101	Sep 70	Mar 73

APPENDIX G

A/A [SIR] FRANK WHITTLE AND T. E. LAWRENCE

Probably the most well-known ex-apprentice, Air Commodore Sir Frank Whittle, began his Royal Air Force career, as one of the 600 members of the 8th Entry at No 4 Apprentices Wing, Cranwell in September 1923. His training as a rigger for metal aircraft was then a new trade because the RAF had begun re-equipping with metal structure machines.

Like most ex-apprentices, Sir Frank, in his autobiography admits 'I cannot pretend that I enjoyed my three years as an aircraft apprentice . . . Our time was largely divided between workshops and school, but several hours a week were also devoted to drills and physical training . . .' He adds, however, 'My dislike of the strict discipline and barrackroom life were tempered by my association with the Model Aircraft Association to which I devoted hundreds of hours, often when I should have been elsewhere . . . there is little doubt that my model work had much to do with the fact that I was one of the five apprentices to be awarded cadetships at the RAF College . . .'

In a personal letter and recorded telephone conversation, Sir Frank said that T. E. Lawrence, or Aircraftsman Shaw as he was then, was 'a fairly frequent visitor to the Apprentices Wing Model Aircraft Society of which I was a prominent member and would chat quite freely to us.'

For his part, Lawrence had a high opinion of apprentices and in 1928, spoke of 'a rising up of a second category of airman, the boy apprentice . . . The boys come fresh from school, glib in theory, essay writers...as a class they are cocky. Remember that we, the enlisted men have all been cowed . . . In the old days' Lawrence emphasized, 'men had weekly to strip off boots and socks, and expose their feet for an officer's inspection. An ex-boy'd kick you in the mouth, as you bent down to look . . . The ex-boys are professionally in the R.A.F as a privilege, making it their home.[1]

Lawrence considered that his fifteen months at Cranwell in 1925/6, was one of the two golden periods of his life (the second was Carchemish).[2] On two days in March 1926 he prepared the abridged version of *Seven Pillars of Wisdom*, (published one year later as *Revolt in the Desert*, to defray the printing costs of the larger volume). It is of interest that in this work he was assisted by an aircraft apprentice Dick Knowles (son of Pat Knowles his Clouds Hill neighbour) and A C Miller, who acting as secretaries for him completed this work in about seven hours.[3]

Sir Frank explained that Lawrence's visits to the Model Aircraft Society at Cranwell was to speak with an aircraftman named Haines, also a member of the Society, who had been in the next bed to Lawrence while stationed at the Recruits Depot, Uxbridge. One day, Haines who had already told them quite a bit about Lawrence, came into the club and in an excited way said 'that bloody man Lawrence is back'. And, added Sir Frank, 'so we knew about it and it was soon all round the camp'.

On another occasion he recalls seeing Lawrence 'in 'B' Flight while he was making arrangements to be flown to RAF Halton for a model aircraft competition.' On entering the flight office he did not know that the flight clerk was Lawrence, who asked him, very aimably, 'What can I do for you, child ?'

'He always treated us as children,' commented Sir Frank, but 'the incident that I remember best 'is that a 12-year old girl friend of mine asked me to get his autograph and he obliged me by giving three names – Lawrence, Ross and Shaw, but mystified me by saying that none of them was his real one – a fact on which he would not enlarge . . . the conversation went something like this – I asked him whether he would give me his autograph – he replied 'Certainly, which one would you like?' I said 'The real one please'; he said 'I am afraid you cannot have that', so I said 'Won't you write T. E. Lawrence?' He said 'Certainly' and then gave me the three autographs.'

While an apprentice, Whittle constructed a large model aircraft having a wing span of more than ten feet, powered by a two-stroke petrol engine. The design, drawings and wooden jigs for the model were made by several apprentices headed by Whittle. The engine was made by a laboratory assistant and only the two sparking plugs had to be purchased. The model should have flown about a fortnight before the entry passed out but at the request of the CO, Wg Cdr R J F Barton, the maiden flight was postponed pending the visit of the Under Secretary of State, Sir Philip Sassoon. While the engine was being tested before the demonstration, both plugs failed. 'Possibly my strong prejudice against piston engines dates from this event' commented Sir Frank.

In closing his account of life as an apprentice, before going on to the Cadet College also at Cranwell, Whittle wrote, 'My cadetship was very nearly a near miss, because five were to be awarded and I passed out sixth. Unfortunately for him, but fortunately for me, the apprentice who had passed out top failed his medical examination and so I just scraped in.'

Before leaving the apprentices wing for the last time, he met the Squadron Sergeant Major who felt sure that Whittle had a record of undetected crime and had often tried to catch him out. The Sergeant Major grunted 'I suppose next time I see you I shall have to stand to attention and say 'Sir'.' Whittle did not reply, contenting himself with 'a happy grin'.

Whittle commented that four of the five aircraft apprentices selected for cadetships passed out in the first seven from the RAF College.[4]

A/A (Sir) Frank Whittle at No 4 Apprentices' Wing, RAF Cranwell.
(Photograph, Sir Frank Whittle.)
Reproduced by permission of Sir Frank Whittle from
Jet, the story of a pioneer, 1957.

1 T. E. Lawrence, *The Mint*, 1955, pp 195/196
2 Mack, op cit. p 355; *Letters*, op cit, p 518
3 V. M. Thompson, *Not a suitable hobby for an airman*, Orchard Books,1986, p 37
4 Sir Frank Whittle; *Jet, the story of a pioneer*, London,1957, pp 12-14

162

APPENDIX H

APPRENTICE TRAINING AT RAF COSFORD

The history of apprentice training at RAF Cosford, in the same way as that of RAF Cranwell, is closely linked with that of RAF Halton. The last entry of apprentices in the Royal Air Force, No 155 Entry, the second (and last) entry to train as Engineering Technicians Avionics, graduated at RAF Cosford on 7 October 1993. The reviewing officer at the graduation parade was Air Marshal Sir Eric Dunn KBE CB BEM, an ex-apprentice who rose to become Chief Engineer of the RAF.

By early 1937 it had become clear that more technicians would be required for the RAF. As a result it was decided that a No 2 School of Technical Training should be set up at Cosford near Wolverhampton. To house the apprentices, designs were made for four modern barrack blocks to be named Fulton, Brancker, Salmon and Samson; in the event, only the first named block was built. At the same time, volunteers from the civilian instructional staff at RAF Halton were called for to transfer to Cosford. An 'opening up' party from RAF Halton under the command of Sdn Ldr A C Francis AFC arrived at Cosford on 15 July 1938. The first Commanding Officer, Gp Capt W J Y Guilfoyle OBE MC took up residence on 21 July 1938.

Meanwhile the planned No 1 (Apprentice) Wing [Cosford] had been formed at Halton comprising 770 'mechanical' apprentices of whom 40 were Naval Air Apprentices. These members of No 1 Wing who returned from leave direct to Cosford began training on 4 August 1938. By October that year, plans were in hand for the formation of a second apprentice wing to train Flight Mechanics and Flight Riggers. No 2 (Apprentices) Wing with 594 apprentices formed on a three-squadron basis on 6 January 1939. By this date about 1,400 apprentices were under training at RAF Cosford.

On 8 June Sir Kingsley Wood, the Secretary of State for Air, visited the station where he met some of the 3,500 apprentices, trainees and staff. Four days later the public was invited to attend a ceremonial parade at RAF Cosford where the full station strength turned out for their benefit. The first passing out parade at RAF Cosford took place on 25 July when over 1,500 apprentices paraded to honour the 70 apprentices graduating from No 2 School of Technical Training. Two apprentices were selected for cadetships for officer training to the RAF College Cranwell.

Following the outbreak of World War II, apprentice training was discontinued to enable Flight Mechanics and Flight Riggers to be trained on comparatively short courses. The complete rundown of apprentice training at Cosford took about six months but in January 1940, 643 Aircraft Apprentices and 80 Naval Air Apprentices were still being trained as Fitter II or Fitter/Armourers in No 1 (Apprentices) Wing. Apprentice training finally ended on 15 March 1940 with the graduation of 176 Fitter IIE's and 92 Fitter/Armourers from Nos 1 and 2 Wings. Both the Wings were disbanded and reformed to accommodate 900 airmen trainees.

Post-war apprentice training at Cosford
With the adaptation of the training pattern in the Royal Air Force to match changes in the trade structure, apprentice training at RAF Cosford resumed on 4 September 1964. The new scheme provided for Craft Apprentices to take a one-year course in photography or telegraphy, or a two-year course as electronic fitters. Technician Apprentices underwent a three-year training course as Electronic Technicians (Air).

From 1965 the training of apprentices predominated at RAF Cosford where at its peak nearly one thousand boys were undergoing apprenticeship training. Most of these were two year Craft Apprentices with about a hundred attending a one-year mechanics apprenticeship and the same number a technician apprenticeship. Training consisted of academic studies in mathematics, physics and liberal studies, together with theoretical and practical work on equipment and fault diagnosis and maintenance of aircraft.

General service training included resource and initiative training which until 1968 largely consisted of Summer Camps held in an area some 25 miles from Snowdonia. In August that year and again in 1969 small groups of apprentices with accompanying NCO's and officers made up expeditions to cross the Alps and to the Hudson Bay area of Canada. From 1962 exchange visits were arranged with the French Air Apprentice School at Saintes.

Important ceremonial duties included participation of the Apprentice Band at the Royal Tournament, Earles Court in 1969 and in 1971. One important event was the conferment of the Freedom of Entry to the County Borough of Wolverhampton to RAF Cosford which took place on 12 October 1967 (ten years after the similar honour accorded by Aylesbury to RAF Halton). The Station Commander Gp Capt H A J Mills OBE represented the station, comprising three squadrons, the apprentice band together with the Queen's Colour and Escort Squadron and No 4 Regional Band, at the ceremony in front of the Town Hall.

Only ten years after the resumption of apprentice training at Cosford the one and two year craft apprenticeships were phased out so that by July 1973 the Apprentice Wing was reduced to Squadron level. The three-year technician apprentices continued training at RAF Cosford until March 1976 when they were replaced by the new three-year apprenticeships in the trades of Electronic Technician (Air Communications and Air Radar) and Electronic Technician (Navigation Instruments). The Apprentices whose training had concentrated in the more specialized areas of electronics graduated with the rank of Junior Technician as either L Tech NI or LTech AC/AR.

This scheme continued until 1989 when it was decided that Nos 154 and 155 Entries would be the last in the three-year apprenticeship scheme. Apprentices were now required to master all three elements of the Avionics specialization – air communications, air radar and flight systems. For the first time in the history of the RAF apprentice scheme, apprentices completed a 3½ year training course before graduating as Junior Technicians with a BTEC HNC qualification. As mentioned in Chapter 8 above, the 7th October 1993 constituted an historic occasion when the last apprentice entry, No 155 – the corresponding No 155 Entry graduated from Halton on 24th June 1993 – to be trained in the Royal Air Force graduated from RAF Cosford.

APPENDIX I

RAF HALTON – ENTRY NUMBERS AND INTAKES

The Aircraft Apprentice Scheme totals shown below do not take account wastage and must be adjusted to allow for premature discharge, failure to pass out, reassignment to a junior entry, etc. With the planned entry of overseas apprentices in post-war Halton, each country was assigned a block of service numbers prefixed by the initial letter of the country. Except for entry numbers 35 to 48 (referred to above in the Introduction) most Entries completed a three-year apprenticeship. The final graduation of No 155 Entry took place at Halton in June 1993 followed by that at Cosford in October 1993.

Entry Number	Highest and Lowest Service Numbers		Arrival Date	Annual Totals
1	335282	335521	Feb 20	541
2	335582	335882	Sep 20	
3	361606	361779	Jan 21	579
4	361820	362224	Sep 21	
5	362249	362739	Jan 22	1034
6	362790	363332	Sep 22	
7	363338	363790	Jan 23	1113
8	363793	364452	Sep 23	
9	364462	365117	Jan 24	1222
10	365127	365692	Sep 24	
11	365625	365988	Jan 25	848
12	366003	366486	Sep 25	
13	560001	560501	Jan 26	1008
14	560504	561010	Sep 26	
15	5561011	561429	Jan 27	963
16	5561433	561976	Sep 27	
17	561977	562392	Jan 28	986
18	562395	562964	Sep 28	

Entry Number	Highest and Lowest Service Numbers		Arrival Date	Annual Totals
19	562967	563424	Jan 29	1076
20	563425	564042	Sep 29	
21	564049	564576	Jan 30	1008
22	564577	565056	Sep 30	
23	565057	565458	Jan 31	787
24	565459	565843	Sep 31	
25	564844	566009	Jan 32	398
26	566010	566241	Sep 32	
27	566242	566458	Jan 33	457
28	566463	566702	Sep 33	
29	566707	566956	Jan 34	638
30	566959	567346	Aug 34	
31	567348	567892	Jan 35	1466
32	567893	568813	Aug 35	
33	568814	569665	Jan 36	1934
34	569668	570749	Aug 36	
35	570756	571604	Jan 37	2096
36	571605	572851	Aug 37	
37	572855	573688	Jan 38	2135
38	573691	574991	Aug 38	
39	574992	576080	Jan 39	2135
40	576084	577461	Aug 39	
41	577463	578129	Jan 40	926
42	578131	578389	Aug 40	
43	578390	578655	Aug 41	267
44	578657	578913	Feb 42	519
45	578915	570176	Aug 42	
46	579177	579434	Feb 43	518
47	579436	579695	Aug 43	
48	579697	579952	Feb 44	445
49	579954	582215	Jul 44	
50	582219	582475	Feb 45	508
51	582481	582731	Jul 45	
52	582733	582889	Feb 46	777
53	582892	583139	May 46	
54	583140	583511	Aug 46	
55	583515	583819	Jan 47	993
56	583823	584236	May 47	
57	584242	584513	Aug 47	

Entry Number	Highest and Lowest Service Numbers		Arrival Date	Annual Totals
58	584515	584758	Jan 48	
59	584754	584941	May 48	600
60	585003	585170	Sep 48	
61	585173	585349	Feb 49	
62	585355	585496	Jun 49	483
63	585501	585664	Sep 49	
64	585671	585861	Jan 50	
65	585865	586062	May 50	543
66	586133	586286	Aug 50	
67	586355	586546	Jan 51	
68	586500	586872	Apr 51	886
69	587001	587321	Aug 51	
70	587416	587619	Jan 52	
71	587620	587745	Apr 52	732
72	587831	588232	Sep 52	
73	588244	588505	Feb 53	
74	588524	588789	Apr 53	870
75	588914	589255	Sep 53	
76	589261	589518	Jan 54	
77	589610	589803	May 54	613
78	589873	680288	Sep 54	
79	680297	680593	Jan 55	
80	680716	680935	May 55	884
81	681025	681391	Sep 55	
82	681465	681782	Jan 56	
83	681784	681875	May 56	819
84	682048	682356	Sep 56	
85	682487	682756	Jan 57	
86	682904	683162	May 57	1089
87	683275	683834	Sep 57	
88	683842	684211	Jan 58	
89	684227	684381	May 58	1027
90	684461	684962	Sep 58	
91	684965	685240	Jan 59	
92	685349	685538	May 59	934
93	685632	686099	Sep 59	
94	686100	686286	Jan 60	
95	686360	686486	May 60	706
96	686514	686905	Sep 60	

Entry Number	Highest and Lowest Service Numbers		Arrival Date	Annual Totals
97	686910	687074	Jan 61	
98	687184	687309	May 61	482
99	687373	687563	Sep 61	
100	687764	687929	Jan 62	
101	688090	688197	May 62	467
102	688260	688452	Sep 62	
103	688578	688744	Jan 63	
104	688875	689007	May 63	455
105	689049	689209	Aug 63	
106	689262	689406	Jan 64	209
107	0690001	0690064	Oct 64	
108	0690163	0690187	Apr 65	125
109	0690242	0690341	Oct 65	
110	0690400	0690430	Apr 66	76
111	0690445	0690489	Oct 66	
112	0690537	0690552	May 67	49
113	0690579	0690611	Oct 67	
114	8018501	8018512	May 68	59
115	8018597	8018643	Oct 68	
116	8018700	8018711	May 69	84
117	8018800	8018871	Oct 69	
118	8018890	8018909	Apr 70	53
119	8018970	8019002	Oct 70	
120	8019044	8019072	Nov 71	29
121	8019120	8019152	Nov 72	33
122	8019200	8019219	Mar 73	20
123	8019221	8019510	Jan 74	560
124	8019512	8019781	Dec 74	
125	8019786	8019890	Feb 75	264
126	8019985	8020143	Nov 75	
127	8020144	8020241	May 76	98

Beginning with No 128 Entry, the following numbers at intake and graduation have been provided by RAF Halton. The wastage can readily be seen. As from 1920 there were two entries a year until 1946 when a triple-entry system was introduced. In 1978 this reverted to the double-entry system, except in the case of No 155 Entry which was the only and last entry to arrive at Halton in 1990.

Entry Number	Intake Totals	Passing out Totals	Arrival Date	Graduation Date
128	107	68	Jan 77	Oct 79
129	72	55	Jun 77	Apr 80
130	107	74	Nov 77	Oct 80
131	63	54	Jun 78	Apr 81
132	97	80	Nov 78	Oct 81
133	33	27	May 79	Mar 82
134	60	48	Nov 79	Sep 82
135	56	42	Jun 80	Apr 83
136	108	92	Dec 80	Oct 83
137	72	50	Jun 81	Apr 84
138	105	89	Dec 81	Oct 84
139	71	66	May 82	Apr 85
140	96	74	Dec 82	Oct 85
141	nil	nil		
142	70	62	Dec 83	Oct 86
143	49	42	May 84	Mar 87
144	72	60	Nov 84	Oct 87
145	48	45	May 85	Mar 88
146	72	61	Dec 85	Oct 88
147	48	41	May 86	Mar 89
148	72	57	Nov 86	Oct 89
149	50	37	May 87	May 90
150	70	51	Dec 87	Dec 90
151	45	38	May 88	Jun 91
152	58	45	Nov 88	Jan 92
153	38	27	May 89	Jun 92
154	70	41	Nov 89	Jan 93
155	46	46	May 90	24 June 93

APPENDIX J

RAF OFFICERS/EDUCATION OFFICERS (1937-1939)

The Air Force Lists of August 1937 and January 1939, give names of officers and warrant officers at RAF Halton (under No 24 (Training) Group). Only the names of those who served continuously from August 1937 to January 1939 are given below.

Station headquarters:	**Aug 1937**	**Jan 1939**
Medical Branch: Flight Lieutenant	1	1
Dental Branch: Flight Lieutenants	2	2
Flying officers	4	
Flt Lt C. H. Beamish		
Warrant Officers [Station]		
(of which two were W.O's 2nd class)	5	2
WO's A. E. Smith/J. A. Steward		

Nos 1, 2, 3, 4, Apprentices' Wings		**(+ No 5 Wing)**
Wing Commanders	4	5
R. S. Sugden AFC commanding 1 Wing		
Squadron Leaders	5	5
R. D. Mc E.Hart 2 Wing		
Flight Lieutenants	10	–
Flying Officers (commissioned		
engineer officers)	5	11
T. Griffiths still 2 Wing		
E. J. A. Knight still 4 Wing.		
Warrant Officers	19	28
W. A. Curtis still 1 Wing.		
F. J. Smith, J. Willson, A. J. Russell still 2 Wing.		
S. F. Trimm, G. A. Stocker still 3 Wing		
L. W. W. Caswell, H. D. Beaumont, A. Fletcher still 4 Wing.		

Nos 1, 2, 3, 4, Apprentices' Wings (continued)   **(+ No 5 Wing)**
Equipment officers (retired)
   one to each wing   4   6
Assistant adjutants   4   13
   Flt Lt H. C. Todd still 1 Wing.
   Flt Lt E. A. Roberts still 2 Wing.
   Fg Off H. A. S. Byrne still 3 Wing.
   Flt Lt L. M. S. Essell still 4 Wing.
Technical officers (Flt Lts or Fg Offs
   retired/RAFO)   9   9
   J. B. P. Angel, L. A. W. Deane still 2 Wing.
   A. J. Fricker, G. E. Litton still 3 Wing.

Education Officers
Principal Education Officer: 1   1
   Adam H. Robson MC, MSc, PhD appointed
   1.9.1932, still in charge Schools.
   Education officers [all with university
   degrees]   44   42
   R. B. Garrard, J. Whitley, F. S. Bloomfield,
   T. Hampson, C. F. N. Seaman, H. M. Wilson still
   1 Wing.
   A. Gillespie, J. Mutch, H. E. Beardshaw,
   F. W. Clarke, E. Knowles still 2 Wing.
   W. A. Oliver, T. F. W. Smith still 3 Wing.
   J. A. C. Critchley, F. B. Farthing,
   F. Harrison still 4 Wing.

APPENDIX K

EX-APPRENTICES PROMOTED TO AIR RANK

The following list, which is not complete, particularly for Flowerdown entries, indicates 123 ex-apprentices who have achieved air rank.

MARSHAL OF THE RAF (1)
Sir Keith Williamson   50th Cranwell

AIR CHIEF MARSHAL (4)
Sir Walter Dawson   Cranwell
Sir Alfred Earle   11th Halton
Sir John Rogers   49th Cranwell
Sir Michael Armitage   56th Halton

AIR MARSHAL (7)
Sir Herbert Spreckley   3rd Cranwell
Sir Norman Coslett   13th Halton
Sir Kenneth Porter   17th Halton
Sir Peter Wykeham   26th Halton
Sir John Lapsley   27th Halton
Sir Eric Dunn   48th Cranwell
Sir John Fitzpatrick   56th Halton

AIR VICE-MARSHAL (29)
Monks A T   5th Flowerdown
Sir Thomas Shirley   8th Flowerdown
Wrigley H B   8th Flowerdown
Cannon L W   2nd Cranwell
Scott C G   5th Halton
Lott George   5th Halton
Satterley H V   7th Halton
Sheen W C   7th Halton
Stephenson J N T   8th Halton

Worstall W R   8th Cranwell
Nicholls W T   9th Cranwell
Sir Colin Scragg   10th Halton
Freebody W L   11th Cranwell
Pyke A   15th Cranwell
Rutter N C S   14th Halton
Carter W   17th Ruislip
Pope John C   17th Halton
Disbrey W D   18th Halton
Sir Bernard Chacksfield 18th Halton
Otter V C   20th Halton
Menaul S W B   25th Cranwell
Moulton L H   25th Cranwell
Bird F R   32nd Halton
Sykes William   33rd Halton
Bowring J I R   38th Halton
Allison Dennis   60th Halton
Shah Altaf   67th Halton
Thomson A E RNZAF   71st Halton
Wood R H   72nd Halton

AIR COMMODORE (82)
Jackaman C T   2nd Flowerdown
Moore L P   2nd Flowerdown
Phillips R L   6th Flowerdown
Coats R   2nd Cranwell
Freestone L R S   3rd Cranwell
Dicken H E   5th Halton

Dicken C W	5th Halton	Clements A J B	36th Cranwell
Grierson C M	6th Cranwell	Dainty W H	39th Halton
Cooper W C	5th Cranwell	Topp R L	39th Cranwell
Tait N A	7th Halton	Glover H F	40th Halton
Field R C	7th Halton	Calder G R D	41st Halton
Sir Frank Whittle	8th Cranwell	Mathews J	41st Cranwell
Bowditch R G	8th Halton	Willy K A	43rd Halton
Lane D W	10th Halton	Jones J D	47th Cranwell
O'Hanlon G L	12th Halton	Goodyer G C	47th Cranwell
Widdows S C	14th Halton	Strickland R	50th Halton
Lane S W	14th Halton	Milne W C	50th Halton
Marchbank S J	16th Halton	Wirdnam K A C	51st Halton
Carter R A C	16th Halton	Northmore W J J	52nd Cranwell
Fox Leslie	16th Halton	Gladding R E	53rd Cranwell
Finlay D	18th Halton	Goulthorpe P J	54th Halton
Searby J H	19th Halton	Leggett A J	54th Halton
McKelvey J W	20th Halton	Offord R J	57th Halton
Hickey H J	20th Halton	Allison Duncan	58th Halton
Bayley J W	22nd Halton	Evans M J	70th Halton
Melvin J D	22nd Halton	Thorson A E	71st Halton
Wharton T	23rd Halton	Alexander N	70th Halton
Connolly H P	24th Halton	Edwards D.J.	57th Cranwell
Warcup P E	24th Halton	Heard C M	3rd Cranwell
Goodman J	25th Cranwell	Melvin J D	? Halton
Willis C V D	27th Halton	Messenger A D	14th Cranwell
Barnard J O	28th Halton	Mutch J B	4th Cranwell
Holmes J A	29th Cranwell	Mutch J	8th Cranwell
Thomas C	30th Halton	Noel H E	1st Cranwell
Bury T	31st Halton	Pack J M	? St Athan
Turner C J	31st Halton	Spink C R	? Halton
Hunter W D	33rd Halton	Rogers J R	46th Cranwell
Taylor W C	33rd Halton	Williamson K A	50th Cranwell
Burchmore E	34th Halton	Shelley B T	5th Flowerdown
Fisher D T	34th Halton	Bogg R	91st Halton
Jenkins E H	34th Halton	Hemming I G S	[1928] 12th Ruislip
Wilding S W	34th Halton	Vaughan M C	[1931] 31st Ruislip
De la Plain	35th Halton	Vicary A P	[1933] 33rd Ruislip
Hellawell K	35th Cranwell		

Author's Note: Compiled on basis of HAAA list 1992, *Poachers' Brats*, op cit, p 183 and Appendix F of this book – errors or omissions are the Author's !

BIBLIOGRAPHY

Boys' Wing Magazine, Cranwell, 1922-1926
No 4 Wing Magazine, Cranwell, 1926
The Halton Magazine, 1924-1929; 1935-1939; 1945-1973
Daedulus, Halton, 1927-1928
The Halton Magazine and Daedulus, 1929-1935
The Haltonian, 1981-1995
Halton Aero Club, Illustrated Review, 1992
Royal Air Force Halton, *Information Handbook,* 1973
RAF Halton Information Yearbook, 1973
41st Entry Dispersal, 1992
The 40th Entry – What happened to them, 1989

The Aeroplane
Bucks Advertiser
Bucks Herald
The Engineer, 1924
Flight
Hansard
Haslegrave Government Committee Report, 1969
Journal of the Royal Aeronautical Society
RAF College, *Fifty years of Cranwell,* 1970
Royal Air Force College Magazine

ABC of the RAF, 1941
AM Pamphlet 209, The history, organization and channels of Working of the RAF Technical Branch, May 1948
Andrew E Adam, *Beechwoods and Bayonets,* 1983
Sir Michael Armitage, 'The Legacy of the Trenchard Apprenticeship Scheme', *Trenchard Memorial Lecture,* Royal Aeronautical Society, Halton Branch, 1990.
   The Royal Air Force, 1993
R C Bowers, *Seeing life from a new angle,* 1991

Andrew Boyle, *Trenchard,* 1962
J Brown, *Ground Staff,* 1943
L L R Burch, *The Flowerdown Link,* 1980
John Careless, *Trenchard's Brat,* 1982
Max Cocker, *A brat remembers,* 1989
Basil Collier, *Leader of the Few,* 1957
Sir George Edwards, *Third Trenchard Memorial Lecture, RAeS,* 1960
L Fellows, RAF Halton Glider Flight, *Air Clues,* June 1987
R H Fredette, *The First Battle of Britain,* 1917-1918
C G Grey, *A History of the Air Ministry,* 1940
Peter Groves and Mike Hodgson, *Cranwell,* 1993
E B Haslam, *The History of Royal Air Force Cranwell,* 1982
        The Commandants of the Royal Air Force College, Cranwell 1982
Grace Haydock, *Halton House*
H Montgomery Hyde, *British Air Policy Between the Wars,* 1976
A J Jackson, *British Civil Aircraft since 1919, Vol II*
John James, *The Paladins,* 1990
Charles T Kimber, *Son of Halton,* 1977
T E Lawrence, *The Mint,* 1955
M Lewis, *The Navy of Britain,* 1948
John E Mack, *A prince of our disorder, The life of T E Lawrence,* 1976
T G Mahaddie, *Hamish,* 1989
Joe Northrop, *Joe: The Autobiography of a Trenchard Brat,* 1993
Walter Raleigh, *The War in the Air,* 1922
John Ross, *The Royal Flying Corps Boy Service,* 1990
E C Shepheard, *The Air Force of Today,* 1939
Spenser Smith, *Call back yesterday: Life at Cranwell 1931-1934*
Bill Taylor, *Halton and the Apprentice Scheme,* 1993
V M Thompson, *Not a suitable hobby for an airman,* 1986
Frank Whitehouse, *A concise history of the RAF Cranwell Aircraft Apprentices,*
        1988
        The Poacher's Brats, 1988
Sir Frank Whittle, *Jet, the story of a pioneer,* 1957
James A Wilson, *Aircraft of the Halton Aero Club,* 1992
Clarence Winchester, *The King's Air Force,* 1937
Imperial War Museum: AVM Sir Ranald Reid, Unpublished memoirs,
        N C Walton MS
        L E Ranson MS

The Times (1919-1939) – see references overleaf

REFERENCES IN *THE TIMES* (1919-1939)

Subject	Date	Page
1919		
Boy mechanics – training	Nov 18	9b
Halton Park RAF Camp – Churchill	Dec 17	20a
1920		
Boys – Air Ministry announcement	Jan 26	96
Boy mechanics – A.M. Pamphlet	Apr 26	24c
Boy mechanics – training	Aug 210c	
Competitive examination	Sep 247c	
1921		
Boys leave London for Sleaford for training	Jan 19	7f
Entry examination	Feb 22	7d
Boy mechanics examination	Aug 11	8a, 30, 5e
London County Council nomination	Sep 27	7c
School of Technical Training Cranwell (Contingent to leave Charing Cross for)	Sep 10	6e
1922		
Boy mechanics – LCC examinations	Apr 15	14e
Boy mechanics – LCC examinations	Jul 21	12e
Halton technical training – visit by Duke of York.	Dec 12	15b
1923		
Halton – photograph	Sep 26	14
Halton described	Oct 1	23a
Cranwell, inspection photo	Oct 1	23a

Subject	Date	Page
	1924	
Command change	Feb 5	7c
Vacancies	May 1	10e,31
Trenchard, Sir Hugh	Dec 18	19a
Trenchard photo	Dec 18	
	1925	
Inspection	Aug 19	15f
Boy clerks – entry scheme	Jun 18	14a
Flowerdown Electrical and Wireless School		
inspection	Dec 19	9e
photo	Dec 19	16
	1926	
Halton inspection	Jan 8	14c
Apprentices training and exams	Dec 3	1g
[Age limits 15-17 Aircraft Apprentices		
15½-17 App Clerks]		
Lecture to Royal Aeronautical Society		
Wg Cdr C. D. Breese	Dec 17	11b
Entrance examination	Jul 11	1d
	Jul 19	19e
	1927	
Inspection	Jan 12	6g, 16
	1929	
Inspection	Aug 1	17a
Inspection	Dec 18	11a
	1930	
Training of apprentices: Parliament	Mar 19	8e
Passing out	Jun 30	8f
Vacancies for apprentices	Jul 5	8f
Announcement	Dec 17	6g
Inspection	Dec 18	26b
	1931	
Passing out: Sir John Salmond	Jul 29	4e
Inspection	Dec 17	14d
		17, 16
	Dec 18	7c

	1934	
Passing out	Jun 30	8b
Halton [full page photos]	Nov 14	16
	1937	
Results entrance examination [36th entry]	Aug 2	12a
		4, 5
	1938	
Training described	Apr 1	18d,20
Entry conditions	Jun 10	7c
Parents' Day	Jul 4	20g
	Jul 5	12e
Cosford	Jul 5	19d
	1939	
George VI visits Halton	Apr 15	7a

INDEX